Get Good or Get Off

A guide to getting it right on social media

Ailsa Page and Jo Saunders

Title:	Get Good or Get Off – A guide to getting it right on social media
Author:	Page, Ailsa
Author:	Saunders, Jo
ISBN:	ISBN: 9780980541120 (paperback)
Subjects:	Social media. Social media--Marketing--Handbooks, manuals, etc. Internet marketing--Australia--Handbooks, manuals, etc. Online social networks in business--Handbooks, manuals, etc.
Published:	2017 AP Marketing Works
Copyright	© 2017, Ailsa Page & Jo Saunders

Editing by:	Eleanor Mulder, Elephant Edits
Cover design:	Jo Saunders, Wildfire Social Marketing
Cover graphics:	Silvia Tjong

Cover background image courtesy of Shutterstock.com

For bulk order discounts, PR, marketing and speaking opportunities, contact Ailsa Page: ailsa@apmarketingworks.com.au

DEDICATION

Get Good or Get Off is dedicated to all the stressed out, overwhelmed and brave business owners and leaders, who often feel like they are balancing spinning plates while juggling fire.

GET GIFTED

To further support you, we have created a complimentary Get Good or Get Off online course, including a vault of our resources to complement this book such as a PDF version of the book, worksheets, videos, and other resources. It is our gift to you.

http://bit.ly/GetGoodVault

"There is no shame in not knowing; the shame lies in not finding out."

Russian proverb

CONTENTS

FOREWORD

"I speak to Jo Saunders probably every other day. I know about her husband, her children, where she lives and where she works. As friends, we share daily challenges, hopes and successes. The only thing is, I've never met Jo and she lives 12,000 miles away. How can this be? The *power* of social media.

Get Good or Get Off by Ailsa Page and Jo Saunders explains **how a business can foster this *power* to grow and, most importantly, make money.** Isn't that why we're in business after all?

This book is also written so that you – the small business owner – can be brave in your pursuit to understand the nature of social media. There are too many books about social media that offer a 'why?' but not a 'how?'. The reader is left with a sense of 'I realise I need to do this, but I've no idea where to start'.

Using a step by step approach, formed through many years of experience and training of small businesses, Ailsa and Jo provide the building blocks to carefully, yet decidedly, start your own journey. It isn't all theory; there are case studies to explore, so you can see how other people use social media to their advantage and how to move past the culture where social media is only for posting photos of your lunch! In other words, **this book will help you Get Good at social media.**

So what about the 'Get Off' in the title? Now, this is where I need to be really straight with you. If you don't understand what I'm about to say, then social media isn't for you, and before you can do yourself – or your brand – any harm, you may be better to stop and Get Off.

People have been using social media as part of their marketing mix for several years, and also as a way to gain additional revenue. But I'm not talking about advertising or broadcasting a product or service – the way people have marketed since the fifties. I'm talking about **techniques that engage with your customer and build trusting relationships** like what Jo and I have. Because who are you more likely to buy from? People who shout at you? Or people you know and trust?

There are more and more people out there today that get this. They understand why their clients and customers buy, that there's value in forming a relationship with individuals in an organisation, and the importance of referrals and inbound marketing. This is, after all, the true meaning of social selling.

Ailsa and Jo's advice is about **doing what's right for your business, and also for your clients**. It's not about doing social media for the sake of keeping up appearances or getting in people's faces.

Yes, it might not solve the problems of every business, but if you work out how to do it right, you can make an informed decision whether to Get Good or just Get Off."

Tim Hughes
Co-Founder of Digital Leadership Associates
social-experts.net

Author of **Social Selling – Influencing Buyers and Changemakers**
tinyurl.com/gqhfcqj
linkedin.com/in/timothyhughessocialselling/

WHY READ THIS BOOK?

"It is super refreshing to read a book that isn't all about why you MUST do social media. To have two highly-regarded experts say, 'It's okay if you don't do it all,' lifted a weight off my shoulders.

There's so much pressure as a business owner to be on social media, but honestly, I suck at it, as I don't enjoy all the platforms I'm on. Jo and Ailsa made me realise that I CAN drop my auto feed from Facebook to Twitter, eliminate my hated Twitter profile altogether and survive. They also made me understand that I don't have a real strategy and I have never measured my social media. So I'm going to stick to my favourites (Facebook and LinkedIn), work out my plans (more training please ladies!) and then measure what works.

A great read (highly recommended) for anyone who has niggling social media doubts and wants some real insight on how to Get Good or Get Off."

Monique Eddy » A Virtual Copywriting Monstar » Australia

"How many times do you hear 'You need to be on social media in business these days'? Probably quite a lot and you are not alone! But what exactly does that mean, and how exactly do you go about it?

Fear not! Jo and Ailsa are here to help. I have known Jo for a few years, and she is a great teacher. A naturally curious individual with an excitable enthusiasm, she has that rare knack for explaining things in a common sense, non-technical way that encourages you to give it a go. It must

be her mix of growing up Yorkshire and living most of her adult life Down Under... how could she not call a spade a spade?! How do I know this about Jo when I have never met her? Well, there you go. That is the power of social media and why you need to read Get Good or Get Off now!

From the basics of each platform to personal branding and the importance of authenticity, this book is bursting with clarity, motivation and sensible, straight talking advice about social media. Get it and get reading!"

Mark Williams » 'Mr LinkedIn' » ETN LinkedIn Training » UK

"As I was reading this, I couldn't shut up the inner voice shouting, 'I have to share this! I have to share this!' There's so much honesty and truth in this book. Social media is so huge, especially in certain industries, that it really can feel like it has a planet of it's own. Well Jo and Ailsa are the tour guides of Planet Social Media and you'd be mad not to listen to them."

Rosie Shilo » The VA Advocate » Virtually Yours » Australia

"Reading this book came at just the right time for me. I wasn't happy with my social media results, and yet I couldn't bring myself to quit — both because of all the effort I'd already put in and also, of course, FOMO.

I felt as if the authors were in my head. They so accurately addressed all my fears and struggles, and also the mistakes I'd been making on social media, that I wondered if they had a webcam in my office! For the first time, I felt I had permission to admit it wasn't working for me, and I decided to park my social media on all platforms for one month while digesting the book and deciding what to do next. And what a relief it was!

Thank you Jo and Ailsa — my social media heroes! You saved me and my business from being another victim of ISMS (Irrelevant Social Media Syndrome). This is where you don't enjoy doing it and you're not making an impact!

The end result? After a month, I felt energised enough to get back on the horse. I decided to **Get Off** *some of my platforms (I downsized to fewer sites) AND I Got Good at what was left. On the whole, I learnt to execute better and be more focused in my approach."*

Alicia Menkveld » Business Confidence Academy » Australia

"In this book, Jo Saunders and Ailsa Page take a bold and refreshingly honest look at social media for small businesses, and in the process, shoot a few sacred cows. Their advice is practical, down-to-earth, and rooted in experience. They are not afraid to suggest that some businesses would even be better off without social media. For the majority, who see significant benefits in social media, Jo and Ailsa provide an easy-to-understand framework, which will ensure a positive social experience for the small business owner and their customers.

P.S. Don't forget to share this book with your small business connections, so that they can enjoy it too."

Greg Cooper » LinkedIn Coach and Trainer » UK

"I met Jo Saunders almost a decade ago when social media was brand new. We called it Web 2.0 back then. It has been wonderful to see her grow in stature as a social media guru (let's face it, Jo — you are a guru!), and now to read her first book, co-authored with Ailsa Page. Get Good or Get Off (what a superb title!) is a must-read for anyone in business

grappling with the ins and outs of one of the most powerful (and dangerous) mediums ever created. Social media may not be right for everyone (as the book rightly says), but before you decide whether you should or should not dive in, and how, read this book."

Charlie Gunningham » CEO » Business News » Australia

"I believe what you say no to, in life, dictates your success far more than what you say yes to. Ailsa and Jo's Get Good or Get Off approach echoes that philosophy. This books gives both businesses and people the permission not only to acknowledge that something is not working for them, but also that they're not doing it well. They can then choose to get better at it, or simply stop doing it and focus their attention on activities that DO get them the results they're after.

I have known Jo and Ailsa for many years. While they own very different businesses, they share a similar no-nonsense, make-it-easy, and get-things-done kind of approach. This comes across clearly in Get Good or Get Off. What I like best about this book is the authors' frank approach, and their ability to ignore what is trendy and instead focus on what delivers value. They break down different parts of social media and investigate what will give you the best value and how you can go about getting that value.

If you are a business owner struggling to get your head around how best to use social media for business growth, this book will help you to Get Good or Get Off."

Warwick Merry CSP » Master MC, Speaker, Exhibiting Expert » 2017 National President Professional Speakers Australia

A guide to getting it right on social media

GET INTRODUCED

Social media is a powerful suite of business tools. When used correctly, it can help you connect with your customer, facilitate the relationship, build your brand and grow your business. It's also the most misunderstood field of marketing.

It's frustrating to see talented, well-respected professionals and businesses do social media badly, through inaction or the wrong action, often through no fault of their own. This book is designed to change that.

We are living in an era of information overload. Because it is so easy to publish content, and be perceived as an 'expert' in social media, there is a lot of conflicting information available. It is often difficult to determine which sources are reliable and relevant to you. Unfortunately, there is so much misinformation out there, which (if followed) not only costs businesses time, and therefore money, but also adds to the stress levels of the business owner, from trying to keep up.

But what if there was a way to **Get Good** at social media without investing hours every day across every possible platform?

I'm sure you've been to a social media course, seminar, or program where you have felt overwhelmed with the prospect of having to keep up with another platform. You most likely took some notes, highlighted some important points in a workbook, or created an action list. Maybe you even signed up for a more in-depth program, but how long did the inspiration and motivation last? What's often missing, is the research to determine if it is worth investing time, money and energy, and also the follow-up plan for consistent action and a strategy to keep on track.

Confession time... We do not profess to be good at ALL social media. And more importantly, we don't expect or advise our clients to do it all. We have chosen to be strategic about the social media we use, and sometimes the right choice for our clients is to **Get Off**!

Social media specialists, encouraging clients to **Get Off** social media?!? Yes, sometimes that is the best outcome right now, and we will delve into why.

You may see us across many social media platforms, but often we are operating in testing mode, where we are confirming the value of the platform to then determine if it is worth **Getting Good**, or **Getting Off.** We are committed to learning and staying current to ensure we are best placed to help our clients make informed, strategic choices when it comes to social media marketing – both on- and offline.

This book and our training are part of our mission to help businesses **Get Clear** on their social media strategy, and identify if they have the capacity to **Get Good** or whether they need to find the courage to **Get Off** and do something else. What will you choose?

Ready to move from inactivity, or hyperactivity to strategic activity?

Time to Get Good or Get Off.

Chapter 1

Is Social Media for Every Business?

Ailsa Page

"One size does not fit all."
Frank Zappa

We often hear people say that every business should do social media. But is this actually true? In this chapter, we'll identify if social media actually is essential to your business and, if so, the best social media platform for your audience. If you decide social media is not for you, you will get to release the guilt around not doing it, or not doing it well. How good would that feel?

Also, in this chapter, you'll discover whether your fear of missing out (FOMO – for the cool kids) on social media is real, or if it's just unfounded paranoia.

It's a scary fact that many business owners feel stressed and overwhelmed about social media, and this phenomenon is on the rise. Social Media Anxiety Disorder (SMAD) has become a known issue for some! Business owners who are not yet on social media worry that they're missing out on a marketing 'silver bullet'. Many of those who are on it, are acutely aware that they're doing it badly, or worse, are oblivious to just how *badly* they are doing it. All situations can be stressful, and can have a negative impact on the business.

The reality is that only a small percentage of small and medium businesses are doing social media well, and an even smaller percentage are doing it strategically. In fact, according to the 2017 Sensis Social Media Report of, 60% of small businesses don't have a strategic plan for social media, but 82% claim to manage it internally. Where do *you* sit right now?

If you're already sure that you must be on social media, then please feel free to skip to Chapter 2. If you're unsure, read on...

What are my options?

One option is to just do nothing. By nothing, I mean do no social media at all. How does it feel after reading that sentence? A huge relief, or are you still feeling unsettled and twitchy? The most important question you need to ask yourself is whether you would be missing out on opportunities if you decide not to be on social media. This is part of the torment for many people. Do I or don't I? If I *don't*, what am I missing out on? How damaging will it be to my business if I stop? If I *do*, how can I do it well? This book answers these questions and more, but first, let's get back to basics.

When we refer to social media, we are referring to more than just Facebook. Clearly, for a number of years, Facebook has become one of the most popular social media platforms. However, there are many other options. So when we mention social media, we're also talking about LinkedIn (yes LinkedIn is a 'social' channel), Twitter, Instagram, YouTube, and the other myriad of social media platforms that are out there, including various blogging platforms.

So how do I know whether my business needs to be on social media?

Often people love to bandy about general statements such as, "Every business needs to be on social media", or (as I often hear, when I'm working with business owners), "Everyone MUST be on Facebook".

But is that really true? And more importantly, is it true for you and your business?

Every business is unique.

If a business needs to be on social media, how great is that need? Will they be okay if they are not participating in social media? These are questions every business owner must answer for themselves.

Now, it's action time... Get out your notebook and pen (or Evernote for the tech savvy), and answer the following questions:

- Is your business B2B (business-to-business) or B2C (business-to-consumer)?
- If you're wanting to engage with other businesses, then with which people in those businesses are you wanting to do business?
  Who are your ideal customers or the audience with whom you're wanting to engage?
- On which social media platform are they currently active?
- Do your customers or audience expect to find you on that social media platform?
- Do they want to engage in business on that particular social media platform?
- Where do your customers go to review products and businesses?
- Are they on more than one social media platform?
- How do they use social media? (e.g. Do they just have a presence? Do they share content? Do they engage on their own channel? Do they engage on other businesses' channels? Do they engage with individuals? What sort of content do they share and engage with?)

To answer these questions, you'll need to know a lot about your target market and their online behaviour.

Now let's look at your business.

- What sort of products or services do you have?
- Is your product a product that can be photographed?
- If you are a service, how best can you showcase it?

A photo-based social media platform like Instagram can be great for photogenic products or people (and yes, everyone has a photogenic angle!). But maybe your products and services are better communicated through video, or described in detail instead. These are the things that are going to help determine whether or not you need to be on social media and which platform is most appropriate.

What outcomes do I want from social media?

It's also important to consider the outcomes you're actually wanting to achieve from social media (e.g. raised awareness, greater engagement with customers, or leads). There are a range of platforms and content delivery mediums out there.

If you're wanting to build up an online presence, social media can be an excellent way to leverage search engine optimisation (SEO) and also increase traffic to your website.

Creating social proof for your brand is another way that social media can be used. Your primary reason for building a presence may be easily capturing and sharing reviews, recommendations and testimonials. Social proof can be achieved offline, but if most of your customers are searching for you or researching you online, then a social media strategy will help achieve this.

Lots of businesses want leads and referrals from social media, and yes, there are other ways you can achieve this. However, for certain businesses, social media and online reviews are the only way to go. For example, if you're a café

or an accommodation venue, your customer reviews carry a lot of weight, and it doesn't require a huge effort on your part. Most of the time, the customers do all the work

Social media allows you to easily humanise your brand. You may have already found that conveying a human, authentic, personalised element to your online brand can be tricky to capture on a website. Social media, on the other hand, can easily provide the day-to-day behind-the-scenes kind of communication your clients are looking for.

Perhaps you're just wanting to provide a communication tool for your business. If you know that your customers are on social media and prefer to communicate through instant message, then having an up-to-date presence, and a system to manage it, will be your starting point. Ensure you don't miss out on those virtual phone calls.

Social media platforms can also provide a range of business tools. Do you remember how difficult it used to be to put up a video on a website ten years ago? Now, thanks to YouTube, it's easy to show tips and how-to videos. And with Facebook, you can even take your audience behind the scenes, conduct interviews, launch a product or deliver training with Facebook Live. The possibilities are endless.

We have discussed outcomes, but another thing to consider, which is often the elephant in the room, is whether you actually LIKE using social media. A lot of people can't stand many aspects of social media. Personal and business purposes are very different though, so while you may not want to use it personally, you can choose to be on it for business purposes. You may even limit your use to reading online forums, or using the particular business tools that social media can provide, without getting caught up in keeping up.

Everyone says I should be on social media.

Firstly, who's everyone? And secondly, should you be listening to them? Yes, without a doubt, social media has had a huge impact on businesses around the world, but it doesn't necessarily mean that you have to be on it to achieve your business objectives. They're assuming a one-size-fits-all approach will suit you. Instead, could there be other marketing methods you can employ to achieve your outcomes?

My competitors are on social media, and I need to keep up with them.

Let's consider for a moment how well your competitors are doing on social media. Just because they're on it, doesn't mean they're rocking it. If, on the other hand, your competition is being found more easily online because of their social media presence, or they look better than you do because they've got really cool content and social proof (and that matters to your customer!), then yes, this could be a good enough reason to **Get On** and **Get Good**!

Isn't social media just a fad?

In the past, businesses have asked me if social media was here to stay. I would always reply that if social media is a fad, then it's been going for a very long time. Think about how long it was that fluorescent socks, flares, or happy pants were fashionable... not long. They were a fad. Some fads come back, but generally the lifespan is short.

Facebook launched in 2004 and is still growing strong. LinkedIn was founded in 2002, and according to them, is still growing at a rate of two new members every second. I would say they've both outgrown being labelled as a fad. Yes, social media at a micro-level does change a lot, and we

certainly don't know exactly what it's going to be like in a couple of years' time, but it is safe to say that social media — in some form or another — is here to stay.

What if I haven't seen any results from my social media efforts?

There are some businesses who are *not* reaping rewards from social media right now. Maybe you are that business. Although generally, businesses *not* seeing results are the businesses that have no strategy, those who have been misled into a one-size-fits all approach, or the ones whose audience simply aren't there. Maybe someone has told you to be on a particular online platform, but you've done no research and there's no strategy behind it. If you haven't mapped out your strategy, haven't invested in the right training, or you're not clear about your purpose or your desired outcomes, then it's unlikely you'll find success.

Isn't social media just a waste of time?

Without a doubt, a lot of businesses are wasting time on social media, but this is partly because they're just not doing it well. If you're not doing social media well, have no idea why you're are doing it, and aren't having any success, then agreed, it's a waste of your time.

Maybe you've got a website with excellent search engine optimisation (SEO), and you feel that's enough for you. Then, great — well done! However, there are a whole lot of other benefits to be gained from social media that you might not be aware of. It's worth getting the full picture, so you can make an informed choice.

The bottom line is, if you can do social media well, your businesses can reap big benefits from being present. Have you got what it takes to be successful on social media? The

answer to this question will determine whether your business should be on it.

GET CLEAR

Have a think through the following questions and answer them honestly.

- How do you feel about social media? Do you love it or loathe it?

- What are the things you love about social media, and what are the things you don't like?

- How much time do you currently spend on social media each day or each week?

- How much time are you willing to commit to social media each day or week?

- What other forms of marketing are you currently doing for your business, and how have they been working?

- Do you have strong networks offline?

- What would you consider your biggest challenge regarding social media?

- What would you say you have most of: time, money or energy?

Before you make any decisions, let's look at how you *could* be using social media. Read on...

Chapter 2

Business Vs Personal

Jo Saunders

"Marketing is what you do; branding is what you are."

Unknown

When it comes to social media in business, most people think about the platforms they are using only in terms of what they hope to achieve. But what about your strategy, your approach, and what you plan to measure?

In this chapter, we're going to be looking at the difference between personal and business social media, the different ways they can work together to create your branding, and how much of *you* should be unleashed when it comes to business social media. We'll also cover how your personal brand and team brand fits in with your professional brand, how to make the most of social media while maintaining boundaries, and how to avoid some of the more common and costly mistakes.

How social do I need to be?

Social media allows you and your business to be social through the sharing of engaging content and your contribution to discussions. Content comes in many shapes and forms, and should be purposeful, but the content that will most likely connect with your customer is that which is full of personality, passion, and purpose. Your unique voice is a big part of your personal brand, and your personal brand is the key to social success.

What we find is that people fit somewhere along the social sharing spectrum. At one end of the scale, we have the highly confident, live-out-loud type personalities who share anything and everything. At the other end, we have the shy, terrified, or private people, who actively avoid social media because they're either scared or they despise it. Where do you fit in?

People who enjoy social media for personal use often feel concerned about letting their clients and professional network into their personal life. In fact, our experience

shows us that people who use Facebook for personal reasons often refuse to use it for business, and vice versa. They also don't understand how to use the tools in order to do both – putting themselves out there while maintaining boundaries.

If you're using just a personal page and you 'friend' your business customers, there's a risk you may reveal too much about your private life, family and friends. There's also a fear about letting the competition into your network and allowing them see what you're up to.

If, on the other hand, you're using social media purely just for business, and you don't reveal any personal details or personality, again this doesn't work. If all you talk about online is your latest product, your big sale and your next event, quite frankly you will turn people off. Social media has advertising features, which can be useful, but using an advertising strategy on your profiles and pages isn't what drives engagement.

One of our primary needs is human connection. People connect to *people*, not to brands, products and services. Think about your online networks. Who do you love to see updates from, and why? Is it from someone being themselves, real, helpful, curious, educational or inspiring? Or is it from someone being salesy like an endless rug sale advert? I guarantee you, it's the first.

In today's business, power resides in the human-to-human relationship.

Tweet this

"Without your personality and your unique 'you-ness', you are just another name in a noisy newsfeed." @joatwildfire

How can personal and business work together?

To see how personal brands and business brands can work together, we need to start by understanding what they are and how they fit with social media.

"Branding is the expression of the essential truth or value of an organization, product, or service. It is communication of characteristics, values, and attributes that clarify what this particular brand is and is not."
James Heaton

Your business brand is typically made up of your professional online profiles such as your business Facebook page or your LinkedIn company page. It may also include a business Twitter account, a business Instagram account, or a YouTube business channel. It could even be your LinkedIn profile, because you may think of that as 'business-you'.

Your personal brand includes the accounts that are more about you as a person. These include your personal Facebook profile, your LinkedIn Profile, personal Instagram, personal Twitter and Snapchat.

There will always be a crossover in function between these multi-purpose platforms, but it's all about how you use each one. If you're clear on how you use each one to fit your purpose and your audience, then you can more clearly define your brand.

What exactly is my personal brand?

Well, it's two-fold. There's the part that comes directly from you and the part that's your reflection. Not only is your personal brand anchored on your values, vision, voice, passions and purpose, it's also reflected in your reputation, the perception of you, and what's actually being said when you're not in the room. I like to think of it as a feeling that's created through your actions, your content, and how you interact with people. Your personal brand has the power to connect or repel the people around you, both on- and offline.

If you don't **Get Clear** and define what you want your personal brand to look and feel like, others will define it for you.

Let's start with understanding your values – both your personal values and your business values. Understand what they are and live them. Whether you're at a networking event or out socially with friends or family, when you're being authentic and in line with your own values, you have the ability to attract and connect with the right people for you.
If you don't feel confident in who you are and feel a need to put on a front by pretending to be something else, or if you have adopted the 'fake it 'til you make it' mentality, the

incongruence will lead to distrust when the *real* you is inevitably discovered. This distrust can negatively impact both your personal and professional brand.

"All things being equal, people will do business with, and refer business to, those people they know, like and trust."
Bob Burg

Let's say, for example, that you're a new business without a lot of experience in your role. If on social media you paint the picture of a successful, confident, and loud business owner, when in person you are actually quiet, polite and unsure, the gap between who you are and what you portray can cause people to back away. Don't be afraid to be yourself. Own where you are and where you're going. This is why it's essential to **Get Clear** on your values, vision and voice.

"Be yourself; everyone else is already taken."
Oscar Wilde

Understanding why it is you do what you do, what drives you, and what's important, is a huge part of your brand foundation and should become part of your footprint both on- and offline. To help understand the importance of this statement, watch Simon Sinek's TED Talk, Start with Why » ted.com/talks/simon_sinek_how_great_leaders_inspire_action

Your purpose, your values, your vision, and your voice all underpin your personal brand, so it's important to **Get Clear** on all these aspects when creating or updating your social media profiles. How you manage your LinkedIn profile, write your Twitter bio, create your Facebook graphics, communicate on LinkedIn, interact on Facebook, engage on Instagram, and present on video, all form part of your personal brand.

If you have a team of people in your business with a shared vision, but their voice and set of values are different from each other, consider how you can leverage the personal brand of all the individuals in the team. By uncovering the personal brand of your team, you will find that each person has their own unique story and value proposition, and this uniqueness can be leveraged to benefit your business. By really getting to know your team, you will discover values that overlap with your business values and your own values. If you discover the opposite to be true, there will be inconsistency and incongruence across your branding, especially if these individuals are connected to your brand online, but operating without any strategy, guidelines or clarity from the leadership team.

Should I have personal boundaries?

Beneath your personal brand, there lies the personal *you*; in between, there are some boundaries. So, while we can

leverage our personal brand on social media, there are certainly some things we shouldn't share.

Whenever you're about to share anything, ask yourself these key questions:

- Would I want my clients /manager to see this?
- Would I want my children or family to see this (i.e. am I being a good role model)?
- Am I happy for my peers to see this?

Always think bigger and beyond the now. Yes, there are controls and privacy settings on many social media platforms, but in reality, nothing is truly private. You really want to think before you share anything online or engage with any online content. Ask yourself if it matches your brand values and if you're happy with anybody seeing it. If the answer is yes, then continue, but if the answer is no or you're unsure, then stop and rethink before sharing. Always consider what is 'personal-personal' versus 'business-personal'. Perception is reality to most people, particularly those who don't know you really well.

Do I need to have different boundaries on different platforms?

Each platform attracts a different audience and has different mechanics, both of which will impact your boundaries. How much you reveal also comes down to your social media strategy and how you plan to manage each channel.

Firstly, let's consider audience. Many people primarily use Facebook to connect with those people they've already met and know quite well. A LinkedIn connection, however, may be extended to people you have only briefly met or those you *want* to meet, and your Twitter followers may be people you don't know at all and may never even meet. The boundaries

for your LinkedIn profile may be very different to those you put in place on Facebook, and different again to those on Twitter. Your audience will influence the content for each platform you use.

Secondly, each platform has different privacy settings and its own way of managing content. On Facebook, your profile may primarily be used to stay in touch with family and friends around the world, sharing family photos, and having discussions with your friends, but it is possible to let clients in without them having access to everything.

Take your time to understand the privacy settings that Facebook offers, and don't be afraid to play.

What are some examples of platform boundary features?

Let's consider some examples for the core features of Facebook that make it a diverse and highly valuable platform. Facebook is made up of personal profiles, groups and pages. Pages generally suit a business or can be used for building your personal brand. Groups can be used for business, for networking, and for adding value to and creating a community. You can set up a group as a 'secret' group, which means it is accessible by invite only and no-one can see it unless invited. In this group, you can share restricted content for your chosen audience, such as a coaching program you may run. Groups can also be set up for personal communication purposes, such as for notices to the parent community attached to a school or even for family discussions.

A powerful and often overlooked function of Facebook is the list feature. It allows you to segment your audience so that you can post particular content for a specific group of people. This helps make your updates more relevant to your

intended audience and less noisy for everyone else. In fact, privacy controls help improve the Facebook experience all round. You can set up different lists for different types of connections (i.e. 'friends') and name them for your convenience (e.g. School Parents, Business VIC, Business WA, or Business UK). These lists are manually-created geographical-based groups and can be linked by a common interest (i.e. business). Then, if you're travelling to Melbourne in two weeks' time, and want to do a general call-out on Facebook asking who's free for coffee, you would post it only to your Business VIC list.

Facebook also gives you the ability to put people on restricted lists so that they only see the content you categorise as 'public'. This allows you to stay 'friends' with people without them being across your everyday chatter, particularly if your primary use is more personal than business. This can be an effective way to manage personal versus business relationships. Remember, though, this means your friends and family will see your public business updates, which may not be relevant to them.

Now, let's look at LinkedIn. LinkedIn doesn't have the same level of control of content distribution as Facebook, but you can control who can see parts of your profile — whether it is anyone, your network, or first level connections.

While it's not currently possible to tailor general updates to a specific audience on LinkedIn, it is important to invest in learning how to navigate and work with the platform to get the maximum value. To reach the right people, you need to work with what the platform does offer. You may need to search for specific people and send individual messages, or you can put out a general call-out and hope that you will reach them.

Features like the ones noted above allow you to have a business and personal presence with a singular account. (In

fact having more than one account on platforms such as Facebook may be a breach of their user agreement). But, once again, it's important to think before sharing anything, and don't share any content that you're not happy for everyone to see.

Take time to **Get Familiar** with the privacy settings of the platforms you are using. Understand the nuances and the differences between the different platforms so you know what to share, how to share it, and understand the boundaries. Everything you do is part of your personal brand. If you accidently over-share, you can potentially damage your brand. On the other hand, it may support your brand and add another layer to you, allowing your audience to really get to know you. To avoid worrying about overstepping the mark, **Get Educated**, and understand the platforms that you are using.

But where do I draw the line?

Let's look at an example business relationship and how it might progress online.

You meet 'Bill' at a networking event, who could be a potential client. You exchange business cards, and back at your desk, decide to connect online. You might start with connecting on LinkedIn, your professional network. If Bill is researching you, he might follow you on Twitter and experience different conversations with you there. If you're an active Facebook user, you may decide to become Facebook 'friends' and allow Bill to get to know more of the *real* you at some point. It really all comes down the platforms that both of you are using.

On LinkedIn, as a connection, Bill will see all that you publish, share and engage with, and depending on your

privacy settings, may also be able to see to whom you are connected.

On Twitter, Bill will see all your public content — from what you share, to what you engage with. On Facebook, however, you can easily control the content and connections Bill can see through your privacy settings and the use of the list feature. You may start by adding Bill, your business connection, to a restricted list, but as you get to know him, you may add him to a specific list with a targeted content.

In the era of social business, we're looking to really connect and get to know each other; this is so that we can be known, liked and trusted enough to be engaged by potential clients and strategic partners. As Tim Hughes said in the Foreword, he has never met me, but we have formed a relationship and become friends through social sharing and interaction.

Being social and strategic allows you to take a business relationship to new levels, while at the same time reducing anxiety about oversharing and being victim to blanket TMI (too much information). You might share a lot more of your personal viewpoints and ask targeted questions about both business-related and non-business things — especially on Facebook. And if the content you're sharing on Facebook is very different to LinkedIn (as it should be), you're allowing your connections to get to know you on a different level.

There's no need to worry about letting your clients into your social life... at least a little. I once asked my Facebook 'friends' for some suggestions of hobbies, as I was looking for inspiration. Overnight, over one hundred comments came through, not only from family, friends, and those with whom I engage quite often, but also from people in my network with whom I rarely see or even interact. It was a great way to easily invite engagement from people with whom I may not yet have built a strong relationship. It helped to deepen those connections with people in my

network and allowed them to get to know me better – through a simple question – which then turned into a discussion. I also got some great suggestions for activities to take on board.

By sharing some personal 'you-ness' on your social media, you are allowing people to get to know a different side of you. This is a good thing.

As we've seen, the big thing with social media and what a big part of this book is about is the need to have a strategy. Having a plan, being on purpose, being clear in why you're on a particular platform and who you're talking to, will allow you to communicate the right way and build relationships through revealing your values and vision, and even vulnerability. These are all good foundations for your branding on social media and very good reasons to be there.

Although we love and very much advocate using social media strategically, it is important to think even bigger and take people on a journey to other platforms and assets you've created, and also offline. Don't forget that the real power in human-to-human relationships is often when we can have a conversation on the phone, on a video chat, or better still, in person. To do this, try educating your connections with useful downloads, or lead them to educational content on your website.

We have all got something to sell – either products, services, or ourselves – but we can't expect to sell everything to everyone immediately. Adopt the principles of social selling, and build your relationships through consistency and care.

How can I control what others do?

We can control our own behaviour on social media, but it can be challenging to try and control the behaviour of other people. When others share things of a personal nature about you, which are outside your social media strategy, there is risk of damage to your brand and a negative impact on your reputation.

For example, what can you do if there is a photo of you posted to Facebook, taken on the weekend where you're looking a little worse for wear? Although you can control whether anyone can tag you in the photo, you can't control anyone else's settings, and you can't control the posting of the photo in the first place. This is a risk, whether or not you personally use social media, because the fact is, others are using it around you.

While you can't control anyone else's privacy settings, you *do* have the power to express your concerns. Use your influence by deploying the power of asking. If images, stories or videos don't match your brand, then simply ask for them to be removed.

Another risk of social media, especially for teams, is staff misrepresentation of your business or the sharing of content without permission. What other people are sharing on their personal profile, on any platform – be it Facebook, LinkedIn, Instagram or Twitter – and related to you or connected to your business, could result in a damaging effect on your brand.

You can't necessarily control what your staff post on their own personal profiles, but you can guide them through boundaries and best practice, and even introduce some policies or guidelines. Rather than telling them what they can and can't do, be supportive and encourage them to have a voice, albeit a positive one. Lead by example, and provide

your team with training so that they understand how to use the platforms effectively, personally, and professionally. They are going to use social media. That's how we communicate today. So, now, more than ever, social media training is highly relevant to all staff. Give them the right training, give them guidelines, give them examples, and encourage them to find their voice online. By encouraging their thought-leadership, you can leverage their personal brand collaboratively in order to attract more opportunities to your business.

How do I know if someone is talking about me and my business?

The fact is, if you are making an impact, good or bad, people are talking about you and your business. They may include you in the conversation by tagging or mentioning you, if you are on the platform they are using, or they could exclude you from the conversation if you aren't there, they don't know how, or they don't *really* want to include you. Then how do you know who is talking about you?

You could search each platform or use third-party tools, such as mention.com, to find mentions of your name.

Google is your friend. Use Google Alerts to monitor key words and phrases. These could include your name, your business name, your products, services, and staff names. You can even monitor what's being said about your competitors.

Also, use Google Alerts to monitor large chunks of your content and check for plagiarism.

Is it really worth the risk?

If you're thinking this all sounds way too risky, consider what you're missing out on. Is it really worth staying off if your audience is on social media? Many, many people today communicate on social media instead of using email or phone calls. Can you afford to miss out on that conversation, recommendation, or opportunity?

GET CLEAR

Personal brand

Have a think about your personal brand and brainstorm the answers to the following questions:

- What do you stand for?

- What's important to you?

- What are your values?

- What's your vision?

- Describe your voice.

Business brand

Consider how your personal brand connects to your business or organisation by answering the following questions:

- What are your business core values?

- What's your business vision?

- What's your brand promise?

Also, consider:

- What's the overlap between your personal and business brand?

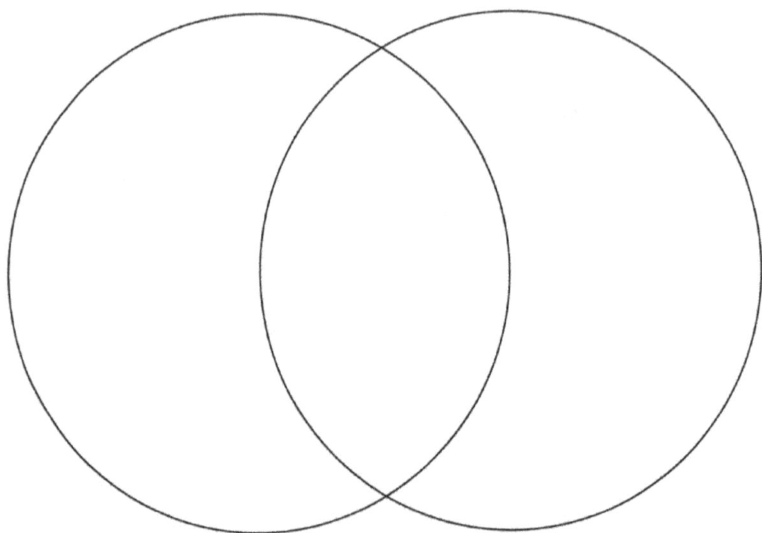

- How can you leverage your staffs' personal branding, and also their voice for your business?

It's a lot to think about. So, now, let's see why it's important.

Chapter 3

Reasons to be On

Jo Saunders

"I can accept failure; everyone fails at something. But I can't accept not trying."
Michael Jordan

In this chapter, we're going to look at ways your business can benefit from social media.

There are five core reasons to be on social media. Let's **Get Clear** on which reasons match your needs and what stage you're at right now. Understanding where you are right now and your current purpose for using social media can remove the pressure to be doing more, and this will help when developing your strategy.

So why am I here?

Is your reason to be on social media simply to use the functions of the platform, just like any other business tool? Is it to create a presence for your business, or to position you and your business as the experts in your field? It might simply be to generate leads or close sales. Or it might be to attract referrals or recommendations from your advocates. There are lots of different reasons to use social media for business.

Social media has enabled businesses of all sizes to compete in what has become a very noisy space. It has also levelled the playing field for many businesses and could, in fact, become your competitive advantage. Whatever your business type, size or structure — from solopreneurs to a multi-national corporation — social media can have a place. Whether you're a start-up business, an established business, a home-based business, a mumpreneur, a freelancer, a consultancy, a professional speaker, or a bricks-and-mortar business in the CBD, suburbs or in a rural location, you *can* compete online.

"Start by doing what's necessary; then do what's possible; and suddenly you are doing the impossible."
Francis of Assisi

Can both offline and online businesses benefit from social media?

You might be wondering whether it's worth bothering with social media for a bricks-and-mortar business (i.e. a traditional offline business where customers walk into a store to purchase). Well, the answer is that both offline and online businesses can benefit from social media.

Window shopping has moved online, and now many store customers are researching online before they even step into your shop, know what they want, or how you can help them. Many transactions take place because of prior online research, and your business being found online along with the information that's required.

For online businesses, which operate in a virtual space and where customers transact online, it's critical that social media becomes part of your marketing strategy. Social media helps to build awareness of your brand, helps you engage with your audience and potential clients, and can drive traffic to your website.

Both types of business can adopt the approach to educate, entertain, and engage your customers and potential customers via social media so that they're inspired to visit you, online or in-store, because they have come to know you, like you and trust you.

Can I use social media instead of a website?

When a customer is looking for your type of service, product or information, it's good to understand where they're looking. Wherever your ideal clients are searching, you want to be there — you need to be findable. That alone could be your primary reason to be on social media.

Many people start their search on Google, others go straight to Facebook or LinkedIn. A website is an important part of the findability equation, but having an optimised presence across various social media platforms, can help you be found more often and show up in the places your ideal clients and customers are hanging out. Investing in optimisation of your LinkedIn presence will help your findability in Google. Google yourself right now. If you have a LinkedIn presence, your profile will most likely come up on the first page of the search results — if not, in the top three results.

Social media will not replace your website and its important role in online sales, but it can be used to help your ideal audience find you, engage with you, recommend you, and drive traffic to your content and services.

What type of content can I share on social media?

Content can be text, images, audio or video. Words help you **Get Found**, images help you grab attention, while video and audio help your audience to really connect with you. Of course, media that has been keyword optimised will also help you be found.

When it comes to images, think beyond just sharing motivational quotes – these have been done to death. Think about the value you can add to the lives of your ideal clients. What images would help or inspire them? Think beyond the

standard stock images and start creating your own. Dare to be creative.

By 2018, video is predicted to account for two-thirds of mobile activity. Video has become a huge part of social media, thanks to the support of online sharing, uploading, and live broadcasting. Tests have shown that – in terms of exposure and engagement – uploading or broadcasting video via Facebook Live out-performs video shared to Facebook from YouTube. However, optimised video hosted on YouTube contributes greatly to your findability in the search engines. Can you afford not to be considering video?

Top five ways you can use social media

You may be already applying various levels of purpose but may not be clear on why you are doing the activities. Alternatively, you may want to identify additional reasons for using social media. So, let's drill down to the five main ways that social media can be used.

1. As a tool for your business

Social media may be used as merely a communication or research tool.

LinkedIn is the largest professional social network, and is a huge database of professionals and companies. Learn to search effectively to find the right people. You can even create saved searches and have LinkedIn alert you when the results are updated.

Used with a social CRM such as Nimble, means the data from various social networks can be used to build a well-rounded dossier on the individual.

You might use Facebook to manage and promote your events, or find relevant events to attend. It can be useful to see who else is planning on attending and engage with delegates leading up to an event.

Perhaps you're using discussion forums (for example Facebook groups or LinkedIn groups) to build a community.

Maybe you're providing your customers with YouTube-hosted how-to videos, or even catalogue photos on Instagram.

It may be as simple as using Facebook to allow people to message you privately. 58% of Australian small businesses use social media for two-way communication with clients and contacts.

Using your different platforms as a suite of business tools is one valid way to use social media.

2. **To create an online presence and make your business 'findable'**

People are using social media to search for products, services, and solutions to problems. Facebook is becoming a search engine in its own right.

Facebook is also a place to ask for help. How often have you seen a Facebook friend asking for recommendations for services such as admin support, a photographer or an accountant? We trust our friends' opinions, and we are often too lazy to sift through the Google search results. If you don't have a Facebook page, your advocates cannot easily recommend you and bring you into the conversation.

So, being there might be important to your business, particularly if your clients and competitors are there; they

could be getting the leads instead of you, because they're easier to find. Building an online presence might just mean *you're* the one who's found.

Also, a Google Search often finds your social media platform before your website. This is because the platform is highly optimised. Also, your page or profile has fresh content containing the right key words and phrases your target market are using to find you.

3. To position your business in the marketplace

Are you using social media effectively to position your organisation or yourself as an expert in your field?

Let's say you're a professional speaker. Are you looking at positioning your expertise to showcase your work, provide social proof, build a network, and to get more speaking gigs?

If you're leading an organisation, are you showcasing the talent in your team? Perhaps you could be showcasing the projects you're involved in, which advocate your expertise. Or you could be showing your work through articles, videos, images, and podcasts. Are you providing social proof and allowing people to engage with you through LinkedIn recommendations or through reviews on your Facebook page?

Do you have brand consistency between your online presence and your offline presence to give a sense of trust and consistency?

4. To attract leads

In order to attract leads via social media tools, you need to:

- Have a branded presence.

- Be building your position as experts or industry leaders.
- Be building your network of clients, potential clients and strategic partners.

Leads can come from paid advertising or from relationship-building strategies (commonly referred to as relationship marketing or social selling). To build trusted relationships with your connections, it's important to invest time and effort in:

- Keeping your online presence up-to-date.
- Connecting with new people.
- Engaging with your connections and network.
- Publishing useful content.
- Showcasing your team.

You will also need to inspire your connections to go outside of the channel they are in, so your relationship doesn't start and finish with that platform. This might mean directing them to your website via an article you publish on LinkedIn or a link you publish on Facebook.

Offer your network content opportunities (i.e. a free download, e-book or checklist), so that it's easy to take the next step. From this opt-in process, you will receive their email address, and with permission, you can then include them in your network for further relationship-building. Use email marketing to stay top of mind, and use tools (e.g. social sales and marketing CRM; Nimble) to gain a competitive advantage across the social landscape, and manage the sales conversations.

By exposing your services within your content, you will convert a sale at a time when your customer is ready. Being in front of your customers — in the place that they hang out, with the content that is useful to them, when they actually

need your service – will put you at the forefront of their minds, and you will have built enough trust for them to take action.

5. To be referred and recommended

Social media offers a range of online referral and recommendation tools. On LinkedIn, for example, your client or customer has the ability to provide a recommendation of the work you've done. This recommendation then stays on your profile, available as social proof to future potential clients and customers.

Facebook has a review function for some page types, which you may want to encourage your customers to use to provide social proof to your wider audience.

On most platforms, your customer can 'tag' you or your business in a post, which could include a photo or video about your service, providing social proof to potential clients.

Let's say that someone in my Facebook network is looking for a good plumber, a mechanic, or a specialised lawyer. If I know and trust your service, I can quite easily tag you individually, link to your page, or share your details with my contact. This will put you in the running immediately, and if you have existing social proof on your page to back up my word-of-mouth referral – in the form of LinkedIn recommendations or favourable Facebook reviews – and then join the conversation in a timely manner, you are even more likely to be engaged as the required plumber, mechanic or lawyer.

Now imagine if you *weren't* on Facebook and this same someone in my network is looking for the same plumber, mechanic or lawyer. Even though I thought your service was

outstanding, it's going to be much more difficult for me to recommend you. Sure, I can post your phone number, email address or website, but firstly you aren't included *in* the conversation, and secondly the person has to get in touch with you by other means. Meanwhile other people are recommending and tagging people or businesses that they recommend. Isn't it so much more convenient for my contact to make the initial contact via the platform they're currently on?

Also, important to note is that social media activity often happens outside of standard business hours. It might be too late for my contact to ring you at the time he's looking online, or your email might be set to out of office. Contacting a recommendation via Facebook allows for quick and casual contact when people happen to be online. It also allows your network to become online advocates for your business, which is where the real power is.

As they say 'first in is best dressed'. Often referral and social proof wins the opportunity, rather than being the best fit or best price.

Which of the five reasons to be on social media fit with your current situation? It may be one, or could be all five. Refer to the worksheet in our book vault.

Do you now see what's possible for your business?

Share

We would love to hear what you have taken away from the book so far. Let us know by your preferred choice of social media tools and communicate with us using #GetGoodOrGetOff

(See the Get Social section for full contact details).

I've tried social media and it just isn't working for me

Maybe you're not getting leads and referrals right now. This could be because you haven't got a strategy, you're investing time in the wrong platform, or you're being too promotional. People don't like to be sold to on social media.

To move forward, invest your time and effort in relationship-building and engagement strategies otherwise known as social selling) Focus on the social part, not the selling part.

What is social selling?

I've mentioned social selling a few times now, and you may be curious about what it actually is. Tim Hughes, who wrote the Foreword for this book, is one of the leading global authorities on social selling and the author of Social Selling – Techniques to Influence Buyers and Changemakers » http://tinyurl.com/gqhfcqj

I asked Tim for his definition of social selling and insights to help our readers;

"Probably better to define, what is social buying. The internet has offered buyers the ability to no longer need to talk to sales people. They can go online and self-educate about the products and services they want to buy. This dysfunction means that businesses and sales people need to react. They can do this by being part of the buying process, listening for buyers, educating buyers, and helping buyers. Since the beginning of time, people have bought from people they know and trust. You now need to lift your analogue world and put it on social."

If you're not engaging with your network, then you're not investing in building the relationships, and if this is the case, why then should they invest in you?

GET INFORMED

Often what stops businesses making the most of social media is their lack of understanding of how it all works. If you don't know how to do social media, invest some time and effort into learning about it, or delegate a staff member to learn about it on your behalf. Speak to us, and we can either directly help you or recommend a source to meet your needs.

Maybe you simply don't like social media. It's well worth either learning to love and understand it, or opting to work with someone who has the right knowledge and passion. But a word of warning – when outsourcing any of your social media, do your homework to ensure the person or agency understands your brand and the platforms you wish to use. It isn't just about knowing how to use a platform; it's about understanding your business strategy before you trust someone with your brand. Once again, speak to us, as we offer services through our team, or can recommend other trusted specialists to help.

GET CLEAR

What is your reason to be on each form of social media?

Grab a blank page and create a row for each platform and a column for each of the following questions to help you **Get Clear**:

- Why you're there.
- Who your audience is.
- Which platform your audience is using.
- What activities and conversations your audience is engaging in.
- How you will measure your success.

Having clarity will help you develop a strategy to keep you on track so you're more effective and efficient.

Not convinced?

What if you've tried every option, have a well-defined and executed strategy, and still aren't seeing results?

Let's turn the tables. Read the next chapter to see when it's best to **Get Off.**

Chapter 4

Reasons to be Off

Ailsa Page

"Sometimes you need to press pause to let everything sink in"
Sebastian Vettel

Is your biggest fear that you are wasting your time on social media? If so, this chapter will help you decide if that's true.

Every business owner brings three things to business: time, money, and energy. Having the ability to utilise these resources in an effective and efficient manner, especially in your marketing, is what underpins successful business practice. As a business owner, whatever resources you invest in marketing activities, your aim is to deliver a return on investment. But a return on investment for social media is often a grey area for many. You may hope that it's effective, but you don't know for sure and are too scared to **Get Off** in case there are repercussions. This chapter gives you the information required to make a decision on whether to stay or go.

What are the risks to my business if I Get Off?

Is it that big a deal to **Get Off** social media? What are the actual risks? Learning about the risks removes the fear associated with the general hype that a business cannot afford to *not* be on social media. Once the hype has been removed, only the facts remain, and then you're free to make your choice based on real consequences you can weigh up.

One thing I'm seeing more frequently with businesspeople is an increase in stress. This stress is associated with the conflict surrounding *not* wanting to be on social media but thinking that they *should* be. These people believe that being on social media is the right thing to do, yet it feels like the wrong thing for *them*. They are spending a lot of mental energy trying to work through this dilemma.

If this is you, your only solution is to make a decision. But the only way you will feel good about your decision is if it's an informed one. You need to fully explore the consequences

of both being on and being off, and also understand that the real decision is actually whether to **Get Good** or **Get Off**.

Imagine how it would feel to actually know what the answer is for you. Imagine you've got all the information you need, you've fully explored whether social media is going to work for your business or not, and you're confident in your strategy to either be on or off. How amazing would that be? Imagine not being tormented any longer or kept awake at night, worrying about whether you've done enough. The decision made, you will have an inner confidence and clarity about your chosen direction. That confidence and clarity is what awaits you here in this chapter.

Let's do it! Let's go to the scary place and have a look at Getting Off!

There are three approaches to **Getting Off** social media. You can choose to:

1. **Park it**

The first approach is what we call 'parking'. Parking is not a complete shutdown of your social sites, rather it's just removing them from public view. You're taking a break. It could be a six-month break or a twelve-month break, or it might actually end up being a forever break, but the main idea is for it to be temporary. Using this approach, you have the ability to re-start your platforms at any time, because all of your profiles are still there. On Facebook, you can either 'un-publish' your business page or 'deactivate' your personal profile. On LinkedIn, you can make your profile 'visible to no-one'. This invisibility factor is important because, if you're still visible, people will notice your inactivity and this can be more detrimental to your reputation than not being on social media at all. Being inactive can give people the impression that there's something wrong, or that you may

have gone out of business or changed ownership. Whatever way people interpret it, it can erode the confidence that people have in you. Parking also allows you to simply take time out and return with a better strategy, more energy, and increased results. Or... it can help you fade into the social media sunset – it's your choice.

2. Downsize

A second way of **Getting Off** social media is by downsizing your current presence. It might be that you decide to only **Get Off** certain platforms. Maybe Pinterest seemed like a good idea at the time but really isn't delivering much engagement with your target audience. Or you might be working on multiple social media platforms — let's say four in total — but decide that only some of those platforms are working for you, or maybe even none. Either way, you know you're on too many because the workload is too great when compared to what you're actually getting out of it.

Perhaps you've done some research and discovered that Facebook is where you get the most engagement, so you decide to focus only on that platform. By focusing only on one or two platforms, you can increase your understanding of those platforms and tailor your social media strategy to achieve better results. The more platforms you have, the more investment is required — whether that's time (if you're doing it all yourself) or money (if you're outsourcing it). Downsizing can be a great option for those who like social media but just feel a little overwhelmed. For anyone managing more than one or two platforms the challenges of social media can be substantial.

3. Shut it down

The third way to **Get Off** social media is more obvious, and that is to simply **Get Off**. Yes, we're talking about shutting up your social media shop, closing down your profiles, and doing something else to achieve what you were wanting to achieve from social media. If your main motivation for social media was to promote your business, then you would need to look at the other promotional opportunities available to you (and surprisingly — despite what social media enthusiasts may say – there are plenty).

If you do choose to close down your social media profiles, you might want to consider parking them first, for a set period of time, just in case you change your mind. When you delete an account, often there is a cooling off period, but this isn't guaranteed. Also, be aware that if you shut down your Facebook profile and log in the following month, it may result in unintended reactivation. Before shutting it all down, make sure you consider the content you might wish to save. Some platforms allow you to download your data or back it up.

9 considerations before deciding

When considering the age-old question— 'should I stay or I should I go?' — there are some important questions to consider:

1. Do I have enough resources available to invest in social media right now?

Maybe you're finding that you just don't have a lot of time, money or energy for social media. Managing your social media requires a bit of each of those resources, especially if

you want to do it well. You might have some time and a little bit of money but absolutely no energy for it. And let's be honest here, if you have no energy for social media, you are either highly unlikely to do it, or that lack of inspiration may come across in your posts and you won't do it very well. In this situation, it can work to outsource some of your social media; however, this will take some money. If you have neither time, money nor energy for social media, your options are limited. It makes sense in this scenario that **Getting Off** could be the right decision for you. Or, again, you could park it until the situation changes.

2. Do I have a strategy, a plan, or a system in place?

Operating without a social media strategy is like driving without a destination. You might end up somewhere great, or the more likely outcome is that you'll get lost or spend loads of extra time driving around and making no progress. Do you really want to invest time and energy on just a maybe? Without a social media strategy, it becomes luck of the draw. It's not guaranteed success. *With* a strategy, on the other hand, you're far more likely to deliver value and get the results you want. It's time to be blunt. Without a strategy for your social media, you are most probably wasting your time. And here comes another blow... hope you're ready... unless you plan to put some effort into a strategy, then **Get Off** and do something more productive with your time!

3. Are my clients or customers even on social media?

You often hear, "Everyone is on social media", and while it can appear that way, there are people who choose not to be on it. The big question for you is, are your customers and clients on social media, and if so, which platforms are they on? If the assumption is that *everyone* is on social media,

often business owners don't even check if that is true for their particular customers or audience. One business owner I know invested a large amount of time on their Facebook strategy to promote engagement and drive traffic back to their website. They had written a range of interesting posts on their blog to share with clients via Facebook. It was a sound strategy and it made sense – not only because Facebook is the most popular social media platform available, but also because the demographics of who's on Facebook matched the business's.

It was only after *not* getting the anticipated engagement that the business owner conducted customer research and discovered that, in fact, his customers were not actually engaging on Facebook socially. The business owner also found out that the customers weren't even *expecting* to engage with the business on Facebook. The whole strategy had been based on an assumption that was completely wrong. From that point on, the business owner decided to pull back completely on their Facebook page and channel their energy into activities that *were* working. There was no point in trying to engage with customers on Facebook if they weren't playing in the Facebook playground.

4. **Is social media giving me a return on investment?**

It could be that you've given social media a good run. Let's assume that you're doing it correctly, but you're just not getting a return on investment. The returns back to your business are just not paying off compared to the effort you are putting in. Like any marketing strategy, if you're monitoring and measuring the results, and the benefits received are far less than the investment you have made, then you should change your marketing activity and try something else that may yield better results. If this sounds like you, it might be time to use the resources that you're

currently investing in social media on a different form of marketing. If you are measuring what you're doing and the results are just not there, it's ok to say to yourself, "Alright. I've given that a really good crack. It's time to try something else now".

5. **Is social media making me unhappy?**

Social media seems to be one of those things that falls into the 'love it or hate it' category. If your involvement in social media is making you unhappy, this is a good reason to consider **Getting Off.**

There are some really great things about social media, but some recent studies have highlighted some of the down sides. A study undertaken by Anxiety UK discovered that, for some people, social media can actually increase anxiety and make them feel bad about themselves. Now, no-one wants or needs that! And *you* certainly don't need that if you're in business.

If — for whatever reason — social media is making you unhappy, it could be a really good reason to think about parking your profile or page for a while. You might only park it for a couple of weeks, you might park it for six months and review later, or you might permanently park it. Again, you need to weigh up what's right for you. But being unhappy is certainly a valid reason to consider **Getting Off** the social media ride.

6. **Am I engaging with anyone on social media?**

Ever feel like you are talking and nobody's listening? If you feel like this a lot, and you're just not getting the engagement for which you're aiming, this could be another reason to consider **Getting Off** social media. There are a couple of reasons as to why you may or may not be getting

engagement from your target audience. You are either doing a really poor job and your content isn't appealing or relevant, or your clients or the people you're trying to engage with are just not playing in the playground in which you're focusing your efforts. Engagement is such a key part of being successful on social media. If you are unable to achieve this, then you are missing out on the full potential of social media. But be aware that if you haven't done your research on audience, topics, and preferred medium for content, then you haven't given it your best shot. This concept fits in well with the **Get Good** or **Get Off** philosophy.

7. Is my social media presence too automated?

So, you started with social media some time ago, and for a while it was working well. But then as part of your time management strategies, you have automated elements of your social media. Have you fallen into the trap that many businesses do? Has your social media lost the social element? Are you totally automating your social media, yet still expecting big results?

One of my favourite sayings is:

"When it comes to #SocialMedia, just because you can, doesn't mean you should." @AilsaPage

Automating is a trap, because although the technology provides the means, without a strategy, it's only function. Are you adding the same posts across a whole range of social

media platforms just because you can? If your answer is yes, then that's a really, really good reason for you to **Get Off**. You have ripped the heart and soul out of your social media because you're not prepared to be personal, and that's what really underpins success in social media. The whole one-size-fits-all approach is a disaster. There are different languages that need to be spoken in many different ways across every different platform. To approach it all in the same way is just not going to work. So yep, just **Get Off**, or:

"Rethink, relearn and Get Good"
Jo Saunders

8. Are the risks too great?

For some people, there are real risks associated with being on social media. You might need to stay under the radar for physical safety, professional employment, or privacy reasons. This, by itself, is not reason enough to **Get Off** social media entirely. However, there are some specific situations where social media provides an opportunity for personal issues to impact on a professional platform – just like it can in real life.

It might sound extreme to mention the Witness Protection Program, but with six degrees of separation on social media, your privacy is put at risk. If you have anyone associated with your business or personal life, who needs privacy for their own security or for the security of their children, you need to be mindful of how you use your social media. The restrictions that you may implement to protect yourself, although warranted, could have an impact on the success of your business's social media strategy. This is because an

impersonal or distant approach isn't nearly as effective for your business.

Less extreme, but just as risky to your business, is when bad relationships in your private life spill over into the professional realm. This is particularly likely in an abusive relationship, or during a separation, custody battle, unfair dismissal claim, or family dispute. Even disgruntled employees can cause a problem, or if a customer holds a grudge. Obviously it makes sense to try and manage these situations offline, but people's reactions and vindictiveness cannot always be predicted or controlled.

Many businesses worry about receiving negative feedback on social media, whether this is from competitors, unhappy customers, or ex-staff. A business owner I knew was going through a separation, and the ex-partner, using a different name, posted negative reviews about the business on Facebook. As you can imagine, social media quickly became a very difficult and unproductive undertaking for the business owner, as they were constantly forced into damage control. Not only did the situation take a lot of energy to deal with on a daily basis, it was also highly distressing. Sometimes all it takes for social media to become a risk to you and your business is a couple of loose cannons in your circle who get nasty, take to social media to vent, make false accusations, or behave in an unsocial manner.

However, when you're dealing with your customers, rather than ignoring negative comments, it's actually always worth engaging in a professional, polite, and non-provocative way. How you respond to a customer complaint can have a big impact on how people perceive your business. In fact, responding to a negative comment in a positive way can completely turn things around. Some people just want to be heard; some people act in haste. Either way, take your time to respond to their concerns and fix the problem. You might

even win them back. Also, if you consistently act in a professional manner, especially when online for all to see, you will build up trust from others.

If, however, at any stage the comments get nasty, or move into the personal realm, then this strategy will not work. So, if there is personal stuff going on in your life that may spill over into social media, then this could be a good enough reason to park it or **Get Off.**

9. Have I lost sight of the ball?

If you find that your participation in social media is becoming more of a distraction than a *help* to your business, then it's a very good time to consider **Getting Off**. I've seen many businesses fall into the trap of promoting their Facebook page or Instagram account, focusing on getting 'likes' and 'followers', and forgetting all about the main game of business, which is to sell your products and services. Marketing activity that doesn't lead to sales is not the right activity for you!

Whether directly or indirectly, social media can make an impact on sales for your products and services. However, you're not helping your bottom line if — rather than measuring the number of sales you actually make and where exactly the sale came from — you're only measuring the number of 'likes' and 'follows' you get that may or may not lead to sales. To centre all your marketing activities around building your social media platform, rather than building your actual business, can be a convenient distraction, and could also be seen as egotistical. Yes, it might feel like you're working towards building your business, but without a proven strategy for building relationships and selling your products and services through your social media platforms, your efforts are wasted. Success of your online business platforms doesn't always translate to success in business.

Just because you have three thousand 'likes' or 'follows' doesn't automatically mean you will increase the sales for your business. Only when combined with a good social media strategy, and the resources available to put into implementing the strategy, will sales result.

Ready to Get Off?

You have just read nine huge reasons why you should consider **Getting Off** social media. How are you feeling? Twitchy? Relieved? Determined to do better? Or none of these? Maybe you're thinking, "Surely *some* social media is better than nothing!" If you *are* thinking that, then you're not alone.

One of the major reasons businesses **Get On** social media is because they worry that if they don't, they'll be missing out. The younger generation call it FOMO (Fear of Missing Out), and it's a common phenomenon with social media.

However, our experience has found that some social media is not always better than none. Even *some* social media takes up energy, and in business we need to use our energy wisely and in areas that will bring results. *Some* social media, especially if it's *bad* social media, can actually be quite damaging to your brand.

Whatever benefits you think you're getting from a small amount of social media without a strategy is countered by the diminishing value of your brand. By having only a small social media presence – particularly if it's an automated presence – your potential clients, customers and audience will see your motivation as self-promotion rather than as a real desire to connect.

Maybe you're in a situation where your website developer insists that, for search engine optimisation, you should include profile buttons for every single one of the social media platforms available. Could it be that half the Google+ profiles fit this category and are set up only for SEO purposes? The reality is, not everyone is on every platform and, honestly, neither should they be. You will more than likely find that big corporates are across every platform, but this is because they have departments and marketing professionals to look after them.

For smaller businesses to be successful, choose only *one or two* platforms, relevant to the target market. Don't try to be across all of them, just to please your website developer; you will stretch yourself too thin. Just because your website has

the capacity to *link* to every possible platform, it is not a reason to *be* on every single platform, especially if you don't know what you're doing or why.

But social media is so easy with automation. Why do we have social media automation if it's not to post on all of the different platforms?

As previously discussed, success lies in tailoring your posts, messages and content to each different medium. It's also about tailoring your content to your particular customers and ideal audience. If you don't know which customers or potential clients are communicating on what social media platform, and you're not tailoring your message to what they want to hear on those platforms, the likelihood of your success is very low.

Setting up automation therefore can be a huge waste of time and effort. And worse, you can delude yourself into thinking that you're doing all this activity, all this social media, all this marketing and work on your business, when in reality you're really not. One day you'll wake up and realise you don't actually have the results, and all this wonderful activity you've supposedly achieved has come to nothing. If you don't want to experience this disappointment, then keep reading!

GET CLEAR

Time to take stock and capture where you are right now.

Rate each of the areas below from 1 – 5. Where 1 is negative and 5 is positive. Determine where the gaps are and what you can then do about it.

SELF-CHECK

1. Do I have resources to invest in social media right now?

1..............2..............3..............4..............5

2. Do I have a strategy, a plan or a system in place?

1..............2..............3..............4..............5

3. Are my clients or customers even on social media?

1..............2..............3..............4..............5

4. Is social media giving me a return on investment?

1..............2..............3..............4..............5

5. Is social media making me unhappy?

1..............2..............3..............4..............5

6. Am I engaging with anyone on social media?

1..............2..............3..............4..............5

7. Is my social media presence too automated?

1..............2..............3..............4..............5

8. Are the risks too great?

1..............2..............3..............4..............5

9. Have I lost sight of the ball?

1..............2..............3..............4..............5

10. Am I missing opportunities that social media offer?

1..............2..............3..............4..............5

11. Who can help me with my social media?

Have we highlighted some potential issues or eased your mind?

We would love to hear what you took away from this chapter. Share your 'ah-ha' moments on social media using **#GetGoodOrGetOff** or by email.

Chapter 5

Success Stories

Jo Saunders

"Success is neither magical nor mysterious. Success is the natural consequence of consistently applying the basic fundamentals."
Jim Rohn

Many businesses love to learn and be inspired by the success of other businesses. Hearing about how others have been successful in using social media can provide ideas and inspiration to improve your own marketing. This is what this chapter is all about.

I'm sure you've seen examples of successful businesses absolutely rocking it on social media. You may notice what these businesses do and feel tempted to immediately copy everything and apply it to your own business. Surely if it worked for that business, the same thing will work for you. But will it?

The reality is, you cannot copy someone else and expect success. Their intention, desired outcome, timeline, audience, strategy — or all of the above — may be very different to yours. Even if they are a similar type of business, actions taken without a customised strategy and intimate knowledge about your audience may bring you completely different results to those expected... if indeed there are results at all.

Why then are we sharing success stories of others?

Our objective for this chapter is to inspire you. We want you to read through the following showcase of strategies, which have worked well for many different businesses, and change up the way you're thinking. We want to challenge you to adopt a strategic approach to your social media.

Read on to gain ideas about how you can increase the effectiveness of your social media approach. If you're new to a particular platform, these stories can help give context to an activity. If, on the other hand, you're already doing some of these activities as part of your current strategy, we hope these stories give you the confidence to continue on with

what you're doing and assure you that you're on the right track.

What is Social Media Success?

When we're talking about success in social media, what we mean is when the rewards gained outweigh the time, money and effort invested.

You might be getting leads or new business, or you might simply be increasing your brand awareness, but whatever you gain must outweigh whatever you put in to make it happen in the long term. Keep in mind that many social media strategies are long game, unless you have a specific campaign that is short-term. Look for both the quick wins and the long-game wins.

Let's look at the businesses that have found success in social media:

The Professional Speaker

Cyriel Kortleven is an international professional speaker from Belgium who successfully used LinkedIn as part of his social media strategy to kick start his international speaking career. As an expert in the fields of creativity, innovation and the change mind-set, he made a decision to take his speaking international and chose New Zealand as the first destination.

Cyriel used the search features of LinkedIn to find the right people in particular roles in New Zealand. He researched the individuals further and got in touch via email to introduce himself. If you're wondering how many people he had on his list to find success, you might be surprised to learn he started with just ten people. From the ten emails he sent out,

five responded, which led to two bookings! His journey to international speaking had begun.

Ailsa and I both heard Cyriel speak at the Professional Speakers Australia Convention in 2017, where he shared part of his story and I just knew I had to interview him. Upon sharing the video of Cyriel's presentation via LinkedIn, one of the people who had previously booked Cyriel joined in the conversation.

Janis E Grummitt said that she was very impressed with Cyriel's approach, and she immediately recommended him to run a workshop session at a local conference. She says:

"I recommended him to Herrmann New Zealand, who asked him to speak at a special certified member's session. I had previously been the GM of that company and so I knew that they could provide an audience for him (which I couldn't). They specialise in brain dominance profiling and training; creativity is a big emphasis for them. I was impressed by his cheeky method of approaching me and his absolute confidence that he would get work! I also realised for the first time that the world can be a small place with social networking. Since then, I have spent a huge amount of time building a social profile on a couple of platforms... I must try Cyriel's approach to get speaking engagements to pay for my trip the next time I want to travel back to the UK! Brilliant!"

That was over five years ago. Now Cyriel speaks all over the world. See the interview with Jo and Cyriel where he shares his story » youtu.be/9K5lBDygoWo

The Virtual Assistant

One virtual assistant has done very well from using Twitter. In fact, Kirsty Wilson of Interim Business Solutions is one of

the very few people we know who has actually gained direct business and most of her clients through using Twitter. How, you may ask? She allocates a regular timeslot to be present on the platform, and this allows her to demonstrate – through social proof – that she is an expert at social media, a service she provides to clients. Twitter is also a platform that really benefits from consistent activity.
Being active, visible, and responsive online, in a strategic and consistent manner, has been a fantastic investment of time and energy for Kirsty. This is because potential clients, who are playing in the same space but not as effectively, are able to see her skills in action. Often, they are consultants or other subject matter experts who are trying to manage their own social media, but feeling all the stresses we have shared in previous chapters and not doing social media well. When Kirsty engages with them on Twitter and develops an online relationship, she can quite easily convert them into clients.

"Social media has been amazing for my little business. Since joining in 2008, it extended my reach from local to global. Twitter, in particular, has been the big winner. At the time of writing this, I have had 276 inquiries with a 47% conversion! I love the power of Twitter!"

Online networking has proved very successful for Kirsty Wilson, because she much prefers it over face-to-face networking. On Twitter, she is able to avoid doing something that she does not like to do and we are big advocates for not doing things that you really, really don't want to do. In this case, **Getting Off** face-to-face networking and instead **Getting Really Good** at online networking has really paid off.

Could this approach suit your business, client base, and preferred way of working?

The Social Enterprise

Many start-up organisations have a limited marketing budget and can't stretch to a massive campaign. This did not stop one social enterprise achieving massive results from their social media efforts on a strict budget. Let us introduce you to the thankyou brand.

Ailsa and I both heard co-founder Daniel Flynn share his story at the 2016 Professional Speakers Convention. Daniel shared how the ultimate aim is to end world poverty through their business, Thankyou, which started with bottled water and has expanded to food, body care, and baby products. They donate 100% of their profits to helping people in need.

Social media, a helicopter stunt, and a video each played a very big part in one of their success stories. To get their range into Coles and Woolworths, they not only asked their supporters to upload videos and post comments to Coles and Woolworths' Facebook pages to show they that they would buy the products if stocked, but also flew massive flags with messages past the supermarket head offices. They combined real actions with video and social media to garner support and build momentum. The campaign exploded.

To get the full story, check out his book, Chapter One (well worth a read!). Even the book is a disruption to the way we operate, in that it is written in landscape, plus when you purchase it, you pay whatever you want. Watch the video here » youtu.be/xsvzYq2melM And see the write up here » thankyou.co/blog/good-morning-coles-woolworths

"If you want a different result, you have to do things in a way they've never been done before"

@danielmflynn

The Home-Based Florist

Another small business who's rocking it on LinkedIn, is a home-based florist from the UK. Surprised?

Meet Kate Lister, who positions herself on LinkedIn as a "florist at Kate Lister Flower Design (Grimsby) – social media obsessive and generally chatty person." She excels in relationship-building, because she knows how to engage her network and reach beyond her connections by being herself, asking great questions, and being *interested* rather than just *interesting*. She has built a global network, and while her business is in a specific location in the UK, she is recommended by people worldwide because of her likeability and visibility. She has also become a bit of celebrity in her hometown because of her strong international online presence, which helps her sales.

"I chose LinkedIn, because although my Facebook page had really taken off, 90% of my 'likers' were women buying flowers for other women. I needed to find some men to appeal to. I find, in general, that Facebook is for girls and LinkedIn is for boys. I mean that very loosely! I am also more locally orientated on Facebook, as they are nearly all Grimsby-based or at least have a connection to the area."

Kate goes on to say that the 'Linky-algowotsit' (her quirky name for the LinkedIn algorithm) is so powerful that she "work(s) it to the max". She also says that, *"While FB is more informal, Linky is my 'try-to-keep-it-on-topic-but-still-have-the-Lister-slant' type of thing. Instagram barely gets me any business, BUT is great for silent feedback on a bouquet picture! 'Twatter' (her name for Twitter) I forget to use unless I'm out networking! Facebook is great for targeting areas and age groups. I'll sponsor a strong post maybe once a week, for just a few pounds, but have never tried any advertising on Linky."*

Kate on LinkedIn: *"I sometimes plan my activities, but a lot of it spontaneous posts that just present themselves as and when. It's just organic (I hate this word actually) growth! I'm too lazy to track. I just like watching my exposure grow more and more each month!"*

"My best results are far more organic than measured. I'm now 'Grimsby-famous' if I may claim such a thing. The result of that is that when anyone needs a florist, I'm mentioned many times by people that have ONLY come across me on social media. I go to networking events and get told on first introduction, "I know exactly who you are, because my LinkedIn community have brought you to my attention". I love that!"

Kate's top three LinkedIn activities are:

1. First and foremost, would be commenting on other updates in my feed. It gets you known, and if the comments are strong, that gets you views and connections, which leads to sales... *(This is how I first discovered Kate)*
2. Next, would be posting photographic updates about myself with a question – not too hard, not too long, but a question nevertheless.
3. And finally, viewing plenty of other profiles, specifically based in my locality. I can search my connections' connections, or just put in the dialling code and find people that way. I never search just certain industries, as anyone local is a potential customer of mine.

Listen to more of Kate's story in this podcast interview conducted by fellow LinkedIn specialist Mark Williams » winbusinessin.com/what-a-florist-can-teach-us-about-using-linkedin/

The Beachside Café

Many cafes are trying strategies to engage their network and encourage customers to revisit regularly. The Sandbar in Scarborough, Western Australia, invited customers to 'check-in' on either Facebook or Instagram as they arrive, then show the post to the staff upon leaving to get the coffee free-of-charge when dining in for a meal.

The owner reported giving away about 30 coffees each day on average, during the promotion, which means that at least 30 customers were engaging with them on social media each and every day, giving the café exposure to their network of connections, to bring in more new customers, using the power of peer review.

In terms of awareness, the small price of coffee versus the large marketing return on investment has worked well for them. Even better, the campaign resulted in repeat business from many of these customers, while they tell their friends about the free coffee. So, do you think this has helped increase their customer base? Absolutely. The coffee happens to be fantastic, and the customer service outstanding too! With the added bonus of the ocean view!

The Business Communities

Many savvy speakers and trainers create a community on social media as a way to add value to and strengthen business relationships. Here are three examples of business leaders running highly successful communities. All three have chosen a Facebook 'group' as their platform. Read on to find out why.

» Meet Linda Reed-Enever
from Business Business Business (BBB)»
facebook.com/groups/BusinessBusinessBusiness/

"Business Business Business was formed to offer business owners a place of support to ask questions – judgement free – and a space to connect with others who understand what business life is like. In the online world, running a business can be quite lonely, and a group offers a connection space for those working alone."

"The group is where it all started three years ago. We chose a Facebook group, as we wanted to offer an alternative to the (Facebook) groups already running out there. BBB has a policy of keeping positive; if you can't say anything nice, don't say anything at all."

"Originally a side project of support, after twelve months it became clear that the group and the way we ran it was filling a gap in the market. People wanted a group that curated an encouraging and supportive space, and the admin team were active in new business. From there, we grew, and in 2016 we launched the BBB website to build on the group."

"BusinessBusinessBusiness.com.au went live on June 1, after the concept received overwhelming support on Facebook and where it notched up 10,000 members in just two years. The website provides an extension of the services offered on Facebook, giving business owners access to expert advice, tools, and networking opportunities. Among its services, BBB offers an online magazine packed with stories and tips behind the face of business, a marketplace for expert-supported business resources, and a directory connecting small business owners easily with services they may require (e.g. accounting, marketing advice or mentoring)."

Linda's top three success stories from running the group:

1. The growth of the group into a brand of its own – it's has been an amazing journey to follow
2. Seeing members connecting and working together
3. The planned launch of Business Business Business TV, due to start filming late 2017

» Meet Natasa Denman
from Ultimate Business Support »
facebook.com/groups/UltimateBusinessSupport/

"Facebook is my main platform, and that's where people follow me most. I think that Facebook groups are the most dynamic of all other types of groups; it really feels like you're in a virtual lounge room."

"The objective of Ultimate Business Support is to have a specific forum where we can talk and collaborate on all things business. It benefits all members so that they have somewhere they can hang out with like-minded people, while learning, growing, and also being able to promote their business by utilising the various themed days."

"I've generated myself over $500K from the group over the last 4 years since it started, and I have picked up 20+ speaking gigs and secured many collaborations because of the size of the community. It builds my credibility when I say I have a group of 13,500 members, and I use it as leverage to build relationships and invite people in to get to know me further. Overall, it has been the perfect place to nurture and add value to people over a long period of time. Also, I know for a fact that other members have done a lot of business through my group with others – so it's a win win win."

» Meet Sarah Cordiner
from Entrepreneur to Edupreneur »
facebook.com/groups/entrepreneur2edupreneur/

Sarah's group is an extension of her edupreneurship business, aimed at like-minded professionals.

"It creates a sense of belonging in an over-connected world where people are feeling disconnected and misunderstood by those around them. It's about bringing people together in a place where they feel understood, and where they can understand what others are going through because they're all going through the same experiences."

"When I first started out I didn't know what questions to ask. I knew that if I searched on Google, I would find the right answers, but when you're just beginning, you don't know what you don't know. It's that unconscious incompetence."

"This group is about providing a space where people can accelerate their learning, knowledge, and skill-set by being surrounded by people at all stages of the same journey. Where people on Day 1 of their business can learn from people in Year 11 of their business. This is very powerful, as people share things you didn't know existed. You can build an entire movement, which is what I have done with my edupreneur term and edupreneurship journey."

"Facebook has proven to be the most powerful of social media platforms because of the unique personality and character of the group. Like a classroom, you can control the environment to influence a certain type of atmosphere. It makes people feel safe, confident and comfortable, and allows them to build friendships with one another through that feeling that you know each other. It's also great for mental health and well-being, and for building business trust much quicker. Where there is trust, there are

relationships, which is where sustainable business can grow. And long terms relationships benefit the bottom line."

"With many edu-preneurs, a large part of their strategy is to achieve a certain financial income, branding, and reputation, so they can connect to their audience and be seen as a resource and point of call for their topic. The Facebook group links members to the strategic objectives of my business and also to my services and products. The environment has created a place where I am the go-to person, as well as the powerful community. This leads to authority, influence, and exposure."

"The biggest success of the group is having an engaged community (it isn't just about large numbers). When people share their journey with each other, and their success stories, there is no greater feeling. These act as testimonials for my business, and lead to word-of-mouth referrals."

So now that you have seen some examples of what other businesses are doing to achieve success, what is possible for *your* business?

Maybe you're thinking that these example businesses lend themselves well to social media but yours doesn't, and therefore, you're never going to be as successful on social media as them. However, what you need to know is that depending on what you're using social media for, just being responsive through social media may actually be enough. If you're using a particular social media platform – let's say Facebook – simply as a way for people to make contact with you, you might not need to have the most interesting posts or amazing content. Instead, you may find that just by being there and answering those instant messages or public questions when they come in, this might provide you with customers you would never otherwise have had.

Don't underestimate the value of being responsive. Relationships matter. Refer back to the previous chapter to identify your possible reasons for using social media strategically.

"Nothing is impossible, the word itself says 'I'm possible'!"
Audrey Hepburn

If you're still thinking that you just don't have the time to invest in social media, consider what the pay-off could actually be if you did put some time aside to be strategic and on-purpose, or to successfully engage specialist support. Often the benefits you get from social media will match the efforts you put in.

Alternatively, if you're thinking that it's only the younger generation who are all over social media, and that you can't ever get it to work, you might be surprised to know that, while some young people have got an absolute handle across social media, they don't necessarily have a strategy. They are just bold enough to give it a go.

Social media is not age-dependent – age is not a barrier. Many experts in this field are actually in their fifties or beyond, and many principals of social media come from traditional relationship-building that can easily be applied to modern technology. If you know how to build relationships in person, take that knowledge and apply it online.

GET CLEAR

Think big, map out a plan, and seek support.

If you are anything like me, hearing other ideas triggers many of my own.

1. Take a sheet of blank paper (or use the next page) and mind map some ideas that could work for your business.

2. Rank them and determine which are suitable for you to implement.

3. Create a timeline working backwards.

4. Chunk down the milestones into activities.

5. Determine what resources are needed (images, text, video), who will create and manage the activity, any training required, and how you will measure the success.

What new ideas have you come up with?

To be truly accountable, share your plans with us. We would love to know what strategies you identify that could work in your business.

Chapter 6

Unpacking Success

Ailsa Page

"Seek first to understand, then to be understood."
Stephen Covey

To be successful on social media, you really need to understand what it is that other businesses are doing to be successful, as well as what they're doing that doesn't work. In this chapter, we're going to find out what it takes to be successful on social media, and how close you are to that goal. You might discover that there are only a couple of things you need to action... or you might find out there's a lot. Either way, you're going to get a full understanding of the strategy behind successful social media, and it will be explained simply so you actually get it. And then, rather than playing Russian Roulette, you'll be able to do your social media by design. Remember, the more strategic you are, the more likely you are to find success.

Did you know that only 39% of businesses actually measure the sales and revenue they get from social media (according to the Social Media Marketing Report (2016) by Sensis)? 63% of businesses measure 'likes', 'followers' and 'subscribers' as opposed to actual sales. Can you believe that?

Often, people measure what they *believe* is a measure of success, rather than what actually *is* a measure of success.

"Nothing in life is to be feared, it is only to be understood. Now is the time to understand more, so that we may fear less."
Marie Curie

This great quote has never been more apt than when referring to social media.

You are at the cross roads. You have a choice. You can either do social media well by understanding what you're doing – the result being, you get to feel confident that you're giving it your best shot and will most likely get the results you want. Or, you choose to do 'random acts of social media' that may or may not work.

Rather than questioning why you're doing it and feeling like you're wasting your time, just imagine for a moment what it would be like to understand social media and actually enjoy it.

When we talk about 'random acts of social media', what we're really referring to is activity on social media that hasn't got any clear purpose behind it. It's just action, rather than action connected to a strategy.

Have you heard of the 4Ps of Marketing — Product, Price, Place and Promotion – which form part of your marketing strategy? Well, we'd like to introduce you to the 5Cs of Social Media.

The 5Cs encapsulate everything you need to be successful on social media. If you like, they are the five steps to success in social media. "C'mon, c'mon, let's get to the good stuff," I hear you say. Well, strap yourself in and read on to hear all about them.

1. **Concept**

Our first C is 'concept' and is absolutely essential for success on social media. It's about understanding what social media is all about, how it works, and what social selling is. Understanding what works to generate positive social

selling, and what the real turn offs are, is vital. It's astounding how many businesses are on social media without any understanding at all of it how it all works. In fact, they're not even interested in how it works, instead only wanting to know how to post sales-oriented information. They are similar to the type of people that profess to be gun networkers (and I'm sure you know some!) yet don't follow any of the principles of networking. Instead, they see it only as an opportunity to push themselves and their products onto others, and distribute as many business cards as possible. These people don't want to hear that it takes time and is all about building relationships. That's too much effort!

You have to *give* to *get*. Social media is all about conversations and engaging with people. It's similar to offline networking in many respects, because it's about building relationships, which can take time. Social media is not something that's going to bring success overnight.

Many businesses will hire a social media consultant and expect instant results. They hire for three months and then review and say, "Well, that didn't work", because sales haven't gone through the roof! You don't go to one or two networking functions and expect instant sales. At best, you may get some leads, but you need to nurture those leads. This is also true with social media, and if you don't understand this concept, the decisions that you're going to make around social media are probably not going to be sound at all. Take the time to understand the concept of social media as it relates to your business.

2. Clarity

The second C of social media, and one that really underpins your whole strategy, is having 'clarity' around social media and why you're engaging with it. Having a really good

understanding of what you're trying to achieve through social media, as well as understanding who you're trying to attract and what you're trying to do with them, is key. Are you just trying to engage? Are you looking to provide social proof? Or is social media just an extension of your branding? What is the main purpose for you being on social media? Of all the social media platforms you can be on, which ones are you on and why? What is your brand? How are you going to communicate your brand online? Does it link in with your brand offline?

For true clarity, you must have answers to these questions. This then forms your social media foundation and, most importantly, feeds into your overall on- and offline marketing strategy. Having a clear purpose for your involvement in social media creates simplicity, reduces stress, and sets the direction for:

What you're going to be doing.
Why you're doing it.
Who you're doing it with.
When you're doing it.
How you're doing it.

3. Content

The third C for successful social media is 'content'. When we refer to content, we're going beyond a written post. Content can be a mixture of text, images, photos, audio, infographics, video, or interactive quizzes. In a nutshell, it can be a whole range of things.

It's absolutely essential that your content is made priority and relevant to whoever it is you're wanting to attract. You must have content in which your target audience is interested, and which is delivered in the format that interests or works for them. There's no point having long,

wordy posts if reading is not what interests your target audience. If this is the case and you decide to use videos, it's always a good idea to have subtitles, so that if people are watching them with the sound down (i.e. in an office or on public transport) they understand what the video is about. In the case of photos, the photos you choose need to be high quality, vibrant, and relevant to attract the eye. When poor quality photos are used, without any thought or care, they can be ineffective or damaging to the brand. It only takes a little know-how on lighting, cropping tools or editing software to make an image pop. Stop using bland, boring, done-to-death stock images! **Get Creative**, create your own, or purchase unusual eye-catching images.

If your content is not engaging, don't bother putting it out there! Sharing bland content, which happens to come your way, can switch people away from you.

Your content needs to be personalised to your audience. That is one of the keys to engagement. You have to be prepared to reveal a little bit of yourself and let your voice and personal brand shine through. There is so much talk in corporate spaces about being *authentic* and how that enables greater engagement. In a social media context, it means being real. And the more real you are, the more compelling you become. Also, being comfortable with the real you makes others comfortable with you and leads to easier engagement. Easier engagement with your ideal audience and ideal clients equals success.

So, remember: even when using social media primarily for business, it can't be all corporate, corporate, corporate. Boring! You have to bring a bit of the personal into what you're doing.

If you're thinking that you don't have any interesting content, or that it's not something your business can do, the good news is that – with planning and strategy – it becomes

easier to discover opportunities for content and then repurpose that content. If you're really coming up against a brick wall, there's the option of getting in someone independent, with fresh eyes, who can look over your business and provide assistance in this area.

Sometimes, when it comes to your own content, it can be challenging. Similar to writing your own award submission, it can be tricky because you're too close; you don't see what you have that others value. In the case of an award submission, it's better to engage someone to write it for you, as often someone else can see the value in you that you can't see in yourself. It's the same in business. Businesses can often lose sight of what they can offer that's of value to the people with whom they're trying to communicate.

Another strategy for identifying relevant content is to ask your audience. By conducting some customer research, you can ascertain what they find valuable, their needs and preferences. This can be facilitated by a marketing consultant to ensure that the information that comes back is objective. This can be a great way to commence your content strategy. To learn more about how customer research works, check out » http://www.apmarketingworks.com.au/quiz/

The key challenge with content, both on and offline, is that you are competing in a very crowded space. Never before in history have we had access to so much information. Everyone is busy processing the absolute plethora of marketing messages they are faced with every minute.

Can you add value with *your* content to relieve the burden of too much information? It might be the way you curate information. You might be a one-stop shop for short grabs in your area of speciality. Are you helping to explain something in a succinct way or simplifying something? Are you providing things that your customers or potential customers

are actually looking for, or are you just being a 'me too' and adding to the noise out there? If you can provide content that is of value, either for entertainment or information purposes, then this will put you in really good stead.

4. Consistency

One way of standing out in a crowded market is to provide a constant and consistent message. 'Consistency' in social media covers more than just your marketing messages; it refers to consistency across the board. Yes, you need to be consistent with the branding messages you're trying to communicate, as well as with your online voice, but it's also important to be consistent with your actions and behaviour, the look and feel of your platforms, and linking in with your other online activities and branding.

How do your social media platforms marry up with your website, for example? Are they linked up utilising the tools available? Are your online branding, messages and your behaviour in sync with your offline marketing? You cannot have a disconnect between your on- and offline voice.

"The more consistent your marketing messages, the greater impact they have." @AilsaPage

Consistency is important for cutting through the noise to grab the attention of your ideal customers, but also for building trust. The more consistent your behaviour, the stronger the trust developed. In social media, this means being consistent with your presence. You can't be on only when you have time or when you remember. People will forget about you or lose trust in you if you're not there on a regular basis.

Consistency in anything can be challenging. Think exercise and diet! We all know that regular exercising and eating healthy food on a daily basis is the way to go, but it can be difficult sometimes to do that! This is why you need the fifth C below.

5. Commitment

Success requires another C word: 'Commitment'! If you're new to social media and thinking that you really want to give this a crack... well, you need to allow a minimum of six to twelve months to see results. Many social media success stories have come from businesses that made the commitment to hang in there and give it a good go.

Social media, while constantly evolving, is no longer new. Businesses who have been using it in some way right from the early days are getting real traction because they've built consistency over an extended period of time. Unfortunately, social media isn't something you can do just once and then that's it. It's a little bit like running a business in itself. The longer you hang in there as a business owner or as a business, the easier it becomes and the greater your success. This is very, very similar to social media.

In order to stick at anything, you need to be clear about why you are doing it. If you feel that your commitment to your social media is waning, then consider revisiting point No. 2

about clarity. With a sense of purpose, you can achieve anything. Keep your purpose for social media front of mind, and feel your commitment to it grow.

So that's the crux of it. That's your strategy, your 5Cs. Understand the concept; be clear on why you're on a particular social media platform and know your purpose; have good quality content that's engaging and attractive to your target market; and then finally be committed and consistent in the way you're on social media.

But isn't it possible to just be lucky like some of the videos that go viral?

Sure, you may be lucky, but in reality you can't actually plan a video to go viral, and if you did have the formula to make a video go viral, you'd be an extremely wealthy person! Unfortunately, though, it's like gambling. Yes, you can be lucky and win, but the odds are set against you.

It's consistency and strategy that get you a return on your investment in social media – not luck. Sorry for the bad news. In business, you need to be a bit more strategic than just relying on having luck on your side.

You might have been told that social media is a quick fix, and because things seem to happen quickly, it's the reason you actually got started. Occasionally, great things can happen quickly on social media, but generally, the absolute minimum investment to see any real value is between three and six months. Most marketing campaigns take three months for results to start flowing through, and it's exactly the same with social media. The longer you're strategically active on social media, the better results you should see and the more value you'll end up getting.

The key to most of the success stories on social media is the business relationships that are formed out of it. Thanks to social media, real world business relationships can be sped up. There's lots of opportunities for regular contact, as opposed to offline networking where it's sometimes challenging to catch up regularly.

Social media removes the barriers. But while it might certainly speed up the process of relationship-building, the process itself still takes some time. It's like going to a networking event. You might be lucky enough to meet someone who needs your products and services; you chat, they like you, you develop rapport, and the next thing you know, you have a sale. But this doesn't happen often. The more usual situation is, after a few catch ups, trust is developed and then a referral to a business in need comes through, leading to a sale.

GET CLEAR

Are you feeling overwhelmed by the importance of the 5Cs?

Perhaps you're unsure if you have the time and energy to get your head around the concept of social media. Or you're wondering how you're going to keep generating new content consistently. Well, it all comes down to the final C, commitment – a commitment to learn, plan, and give it a good go.

What are your challenges right now?

Turn the page to capture what's going on for you right now.

1. Where are your marketing gaps?

2. Which of the C's are you struggling with?

3. What help do you need?

4. Who can help you?

Remember, you don't always have to do it all by yourself, so **Get Help** from Jo or myself, or others when you need.

Hopefully, now you have a bit more of an understanding of how to make social media work for you.

Read the next chapter for some giggles on what not to do.

Chapter 7

Social Media Shockers

Jo Saunders

"Social media is not about the exploitation of technology but service to community."
Simon Mainwaring

Many businesses make mistakes in the social media space, whether they are brand new solopreneurs or established large organisations. You will, no doubt, discover you are making some mistakes and have bad habits, but when you do, embrace the imperfection and learn from them. The fact is, all businesses make mistakes on social media, but until you know what those mistakes are, they may have slipped under your radar.

As we've touched on in the last chapter, first impressions count. People today have a shorter attention span than goldfish! According to studies by Microsoft, the average attention span has fallen to just eight seconds. So now, more than ever before, we want to ensure we're making the best impression possible, in the shortest amount of time, and not standing out for the wrong reasons.

If you're making a bad first impression by committing some of the social media mistakes covered in this chapter, your brand could be at risk and this could impact your business success.

What do we mean by a Social Media Shocker?

A Social Media Shocker is a type of online behaviour, in which a business or personal brand participates, that really doesn't match the platform or audience, or is just wrong on many levels! The shock could be caused by the *type* of content being shared or the *way* it's being shared, or it could be inappropriate engagement with other businesses and individuals.

Having clarity around your bigger purpose, the outcomes for your business, and your strategy for overall marketing, on social media, helps you avoid making some of these mistakes. We need to be socially conscious about our social media efforts because they have the power to both attract

and repel our audience, and could be turning people off your social media rather than on.

To help you identify an activity that isn't doing you or your brand any favours, here are some examples of what *not* to do. These are what we're going to call the:

12 Social Media Shockers

1. **Lazy social media or the Cookie-Cutter Approach**

Lazy social media or the Cookie-Cutter Approach is the strategy of automating everything, and cross-posting to every platform possible with exactly the same message. Sure, you might feel like you've been efficient with your time investment in social media, but what you've missed is that each platform has a different audience, a different way of operating, and a different format. Your message and your language may not match the platform or the audience. The text amount may not match the character limits, and images may not match the ideal image sizes of the platform.

The other risk with this approach is that your loyal brand advocates are going to follow you everywhere, and if you're duplicating content word-for-word, you're going to turn them off and they'll end up opting out of one of your platforms... if not all of them!

Solution: Understand each platform, how they work, and how they fit into your social media strategy. Yes, by all means use scheduling tools, but customise the message for each platform you are using, and use timings to suit each platform.

2. The best kept secret and lack of optimisation

If you're using the wrong keywords in your profile or content, your audience may not find you. By 'keywords' we mean the words your audience are typing – into Google, or another search engine, or into the social platform itself – in order to find a solution to the problem that they have, which you can solve. If you're going to use hashtags to be found, make sure those hashtags are used by your target audience. *#IsAnyoneReadingThis*

Solution: Understand your ideal clients and the language they use – then use it!

3. Sending traffic elsewhere

Another lazy and damaging strategy is re-sharing other people's content. You may wonder what's wrong with that, but what you're actually doing is driving traffic to somebody else's platform or somebody else's website rather than yours, the result being that you're possibly missing out on opportunities. There's nothing wrong with sharing other people's content as part of your overall strategy, but you need a clear understanding of how this content is linked to your own content.

"Random sharing (on social media) leads to random results." @joatwildfire

Solution: Find a balance for curating content; add your own comments to add context and create your own content; book a planning session to map out your strategy.

4. **Being too 'salesy'**

Trying to sell publicly or by direct message on the particular social media platform you're using, without building relationships first, is a common mistake. Rather than being social, adding value, building trust, and investing in relationships, this 'salesy' approach treats your social media platform like a one-way communication tool.

Do you really want to come across like that 'shouty' guy on those rug sale TV ads, where the business is constantly "closing down" and there's always someone yelling at you about the rug that's going for "49 bucks"?

Posting sales message after sales message on your social media platform is the equivalent of a business shouting at their customers. Businesses seem to jump too readily into sales mode when relationship-building.

Let's look at it in action on LinkedIn:

Person A decides to connect to person B. Person B accepts the connection request. Straight away, Person A sends a salesy, direct message to Person B.

Note: This is <u>not</u> how to do social selling; sales relationships need building.

At some point we must ask for the sale, but not in the first conversation, and here's the thing: it most likely won't be through the social media system; it could be in person, depending on your type of business.

Solution: Always think with your audience in mind, and not just about yourself and what you're selling. Focus on building a relationship with your ideal client and adopt a social selling best practice. To learn how, there are courses available » *wildfiresm.thinkific.com*

5. Relying on a third-party's online space

Maybe you've heard that websites are dead. Or maybe you think it's too hard or too expensive to manage a website. Actually, neither of these statements are true. In fact, a business website is your number one online marketing tool. Relying on social media alone is a risk because you have zero control over your how the platform looks, how it integrates, and how it functions.

"Relying on social media alone is essentially investing in somebody else's business."
@joatwildfire

Although micro-feature platforms (i.e. Vine, Ello and Blab) have closed and taken your content and connections with them, it is unlikely that we'll see mainstream platforms (i.e. Facebook or LinkedIn) shut up shop in the near future. However, these mainstream platforms will evolve and change often without warning. This means you have no control over the value offered to your business, which then impacts the value you can offer to others through the platform. With your own website, on the other hand, you can control how your information is displayed, how it's ordered,

and also the style of navigation. (Just be sure to back it up and protect it – but that's a whole other book from a web specialist!) You don't get this control with social media.

The same goes when publishing blog posts. There are many places to publish your content, including via LinkedIn's publishing function. But what if LinkedIn decided to remove the feature? You could potentially lose all of your content. The same applies to Facebook Notes, Medium, Tumblr, or BeBee. You are much better off to have control over a blog on your own website, and directing people to it through repurposing and promotion on social media. And please, please, please, create your content offline first, so you always have a backup, which is also useful for repurposing.

Tweet this

"Without a strategy to use these platforms to direct traffic to your own website, you're missing out on an opportunity to take people on a journey and get to know you better."
@joatwildfire

Solution: Work with your website developer to learn how to post content on your website, or you can book a session with us » *wildfiresm.thinkific.com*

Map out a content-repurposing and marketing strategy, using your social media platforms to engage your ideal clients.

6. The 'Soapbox Strategy'

Using your social media platform as a soapbox to rant can damage your brand. Never forget where you are, who can see and hear you, and who you're representing (i.e. your brand, your business, or the organisation you work with).

First impressions count. It is extremely hard to take back negative comments and strong opinions you may have aired online.

Let's say you've had a bad experience with a mobile provider or a restaurant, for example, and without cooling down, you go onto your social media platform of choice and have a bit of a rant about them. By not considering the purpose and perception of your tirade, this type of behaviour could negatively impact your brand.

More hot subjects for potential rants are politics and religion. These sorts of topics get people fired up, whether you start the conversation or join in on somebody else's, and they can also alienate and offend people. Be highly conscious of how a topic or viewpoint can impact your personal and professional brand.

Solution: Think before you post. Ask yourself, "Does this conversation add value to my personal brand?" or, "Does it fit with the values, vision and voice of my organisation?" If it doesn't, don't post it. If you aren't clear what your values, vision and voice looks like, book a session with us.

7. The 'Island Strategy'

Are you using your social media platforms as stand-alone tools? We've observed businesses that operate social media without any connection to their brand objectives and without consistency or connection across platforms. This mistake occurs when no social media strategy has been developed or when stakeholders have little understanding about how each platform works.

Social media platforms need a strategy that is integrated with not only the entire social media presence, but also with the overall marketing strategy. The strategy also needs to be part of the whole business strategy and tied into its objectives and outcomes.

Solution: Conduct a brand audit. For each of your social media platforms, make a note of your current understanding of your overarching vision, your values, your voice, and your ideal clients. Then, map out an integrated plan where each platform supports your brand.

8. The 'Hands-Off' approach

Often a business owner who doesn't understand or enjoy social media will outsource it, but when doing so, it's important to choose the provider wisely. There's a risk involved in outsourcing your social media to someone who doesn't understand your business.

The issues arise when the individual or agency doesn't understand your brand values and isn't clear on your vision, or your ideal audience and how they communicate. Problems can also occur when there is no style guide for your brand, a lack of brand assets and resources, or when using copyrighted material. The outcome of these

shortcomings is an unclear message, inconsistent brand voice, and a confused audience.

Solution: First, educate yourself and **Get Clear** on why you're using your social media platforms and how to use them. Then, if you aren't the best person to manage your own presence, consider outsourcing, but recruit wisely. Be sure your provider can walk the talk, is up-to-date, and fully understands the platforms they are using. Ask for examples of their work, case studies and testimonials, and don't be afraid to give them guidance.

9. The 'Eggs-In-One-Basket Strategy'

Are you putting all your eggs in one basket? Similar to the Island Strategy (Social Media Shocker No. 7), the Eggs-In-One-Basket Strategy uses only one platform and that's it.

Tweet this

"But how do you know that the eggs aren't rotten or that it's even the correct basket?" @ailsapage

Without testing out different social media platforms, you could potentially be missing out on opportunities. Not every platform will suit your business, but there is a huge risk in investing in just one platform. What if the functionality of your chosen platform changes and impacts your business marketing? Also, consider your audience. Many platforms don't allow you to download your list of fans or followers, and the power is in your list.

A much safer way to work is by having multiple platforms working together and a strategy to drive people to your business website. Get them to sign up for that free e-book, which puts them on your email list, and takes them outside the gates of the platform and into a place where you can communicate in other ways.

Solution: Look at the platform in which you've invested and then look at your ideal clients to determine what other platforms would give them value and also keep you at the forefront of their mind. Educate yourself, or outsource to a specialist who understands the bigger picture and the intricacies of different platforms. Determine what metrics are important to your success.

10. The 'Spam, Spam, Spam' approach

When we're marketing our service or products, it can sometimes be hard not to step into 'spam land'. Abusing your connections may be unintentional but can really damage a relationship with a prospective client.

So what constitutes a 'spammy' activity? Well, it's being connected on LinkedIn or another platform, exporting your connections, and then adding them to your email list and marketing to them without an opt-in (i.e. without their permission).

If you're wondering what's wrong with that, then you need to consider that each platform has its own terms and conditions, and there is also the Spam Act 2003 (Australia). Emailing without an opt-in can quite easily breach corporate and government guidelines.

The second thing to consider is social etiquette. Does this type of activity match your brand and how it operates

offline? If you wouldn't act a certain way in person, then don't act like it on social media!

Solution: Make sure you respect your connections by inviting them to join your mailing list. Give them a reason to opt in, such as a free resource, but do not make the decision for them. Familiarise yourself with the Spam Act in Australia or the relevant legislation in your country to which this relates.

11. The 'Fake-It-Till-You-Make-It' approach

The Fake-It-Till-You-Make-It Approach can promote a sense of inauthenticity and manipulation, which in turn can lead to distrust. Putting on a mask and pretending to be a particular type of person in business (i.e. further along in the business timeline than you actually are) will catch up with you.

It's hard to maintain a personality or voice that isn't you, and when people meet you in person there will be a gap between the person you are online and the person you are in person. Remember, people connect to people, and they want to feel real connection.

Yes, you might be in the early stages of business and lack experience, but being honest and focusing instead on what you *can* do, is a much more powerful way of building relationships and trust. Understand your values and vision, and own your voice.

Solution: Be yourself, while at the same time, be about your ideal audience.

Here are some other suggestions:

- Write your LinkedIn profile in the first person and in a way that's conversational, using the 7-Step Formula as your framework. Bring out your personality so that your profile is a reflection of who you are.
- Make sure that everything you say is consistent and on-brand, and that you've got the same look, feel and voice across all platforms. This is much more easily managed when you just be yourself.
- Write with your audience in mind. So, rather than focusing on your *own* needs, achievements or expectations, which can be interpreted as narcissistic or disconnected, write with the problems of your ideal client in mind, so they feel as if you're talking to them. They don't really care about what you do, how you work, or what you sell. They care only about how you can help *them.*

12. The disconnected or disjointed organisation

When Facebook became popular, some companies decided to ban their staff from using social media at work. This was because they didn't see it as useful in an overall business context. Now, we have the opposite problem. Organisations encourage the use of social media for business purposes, but with no direction or guidelines, this results in an inconsistent ad-hoc representation of your business. Without a social media policy, your *staff* are deciding how to represent your business and brand. Would you let your staff represent you in the media without any guidance?

LinkedIn is the largest running professional social media network and is used in some way by most professionals, either for career enhancement, business networking or marketing. While effective for individuals, LinkedIn can

pose a risk for organisations who rely on their network of team members to drive their business.

If a staff member leaves your organisation, they take their 'connections' with them, and because the relationship with those connections will most likely be with them (and them alone), the business relationship will disintegrate. It can be useful, therefore, for organisations to encourage engagement *off* the platform, bringing them on a journey into the brand, and keeping them connected to others in the organisation for future business.

Recruiters, employers, strategic partners, customers and clients aren't just looking at your website or LinkedIn presence; savvy researchers will look across the whole social media landscape. Personal social media can negatively impact your brand. I'm sure we've all seen inappropriate photos or comments that really don't belong in the public eye – alcohol and social media don't mix! If the person you're wanting to impress finds something about you or a team member that doesn't quite fit your professional brand, then they may question your credibility.

Solution: Whether you're a large multi-national organisation or a small business, it's important to consider how team members could be representing your brand. You cannot (and should not) try to control them or their network, but lead by example and provide guidelines and training to socially empower them.

Take little steps to Get Good or Get off

So, there we have it — the 12 Social Media Shockers. You might be thinking that this all sounds like a lot to consider and it will take a lot of time and effort to retract bad habits. You might also be thinking that something is better than nothing and that having your Hootsuite account blasting out

one message to all your different networks is better than doing nothing.

As we've mentioned before, 'random acts of social media' without thought or purpose can actually do damage to your brand. If you're not going to **Get Good** on social media, potentially damaging your brand, you may be better to **Get Off** for the sake of your organisation or business.

If you believe that all you need is a Facebook page, you must consider if one tool is enough and if your audience is actually there. Facebook is designed to be a social tool, not a direct selling tool. We talk about social selling, but don't focus on the selling part. Social selling is about connections, relationship-building, and engagement.

Your premium selling tool is your website, not your Facebook profile. Your website is a key tool in your marketing tool kit, and a serious business will not sacrifice a website. Your social media platforms, on the other hand, are relationship and engagement tools, driving your customers to your website. And, using this approach, you will sell when the time is right, because in a relationship, timing matters.

If you think that your receptionist or a general virtual assistant is better suited to managing your social media, website, and email list, it's important to have an overarching strategy, education in place, and a shared commitment. Don't outsource without providing some training, and don't leave the strategy to an outsider. If you're stuck for time and resources, outsource to a specialist. A specialist can help you create your strategy, will know how to operate these platforms and tools, and will take the time to understand your requirements.

GET CLEAR

Now that you understand more about the mistakes you can make on social media, you can consider if your social media activity is serving you in a way that matches your brand and benefits your business or if it's scaring your potential clients away.

Rather than risking your reputation and alienating your audience, step back and have a think about what small steps you can take to **Get Good** or just **Get Off.**

- What is working well?

- What needs attention?

If you've been guilty of being a Social Media Shocker, please don't stress. Improvement starts with awareness. Book a session with us to **Get Clear** on what now is the best path forward for you.

Chapter 8

Get Strategic

Jo Saunders

"The best thing you can do is the right thing. The next best thing is the wrong thing and the worst is nothing."
Theodore Roosevelt

This chapter will give you clarity around how to develop your social media strategy. By creating a social media strategy, you'll not only save time and energy, but also streamline your activities so they're directed more towards business results. And more importantly, you'll learn to love the social media you're opting into.

"Culture eats strategy for breakfast."
Peter Drucker

Whether you're a solopreneur, a consultant, a speaker, SME, or multi-national business, it's the culture of your organisation that connects to people. You can communicate your culture to your customers through your social media content, along with an overarching strategy. Without a strategy, you're playing 'social media roulette' and gambling with your time, financial investment, and reputation.

Because many social media platforms are free to use, many businesses don't allocate resources, staff, or budget to create or manage them. But without investing some time and effort into your brand foundations and strategy, you're really putting your bet on 'Black 12' and hoping by chance it comes up.

By 'strategy' we mean having a defined plan that works positively for your business, and requiring a commitment from you and your staff to execute and manage. With strategy must come a willingness to learn how to create and execute, or at the very least, a commitment to outsource to the right expert.

Here are seven question to ask when creating a social media strategy:

1. **Why?**

It all starts with why you are using social media. What's your purpose, your business vision, and your mission? What are your values, and how do they connect to the big picture?

Simon Sinek developed the concept of the 'golden circle', which all starts with a 'why'. He says that people connect easier to *why* you do what you do than *what* it is that you do. Read his book, Start With Why, and watch his Ted Talk » youtu.be/qp0HIF3SfI4

It's important to **Get Clear** on your why before you actually **Get On** social media. This is so that everything you do on social media is connected to your purpose for being there.

2. **Who?**

Next, you must define your audience. Who are your ideal clients? Who are you talking to online? It might sound obvious, but many people just don't have that clarity. Having an idea about who your audience is — their demographic, their geographic, where they hang out, and even what keeps them up at night — is crucial to your strategy.

Understanding the 'who' will mean you can invest the right amount of effort to be top of mind when they need a product or service. If you're in the space they're in and talking about the stuff that matters, you'll be more likely considered as a solution to their problems. Build personas to represent your ideal market, and seek help creating them if you're unsure.

3. Where?

'Where' comes down to your platform selection. Where do these people hang out online, and where are you prepared to invest time and effort?

If you hate Facebook with a passion and your audience clearly aren't there, then there's no point having a Facebook page. On the other hand, if you hate Facebook with a passion but your audience are guaranteed to be there, you need to put the dislike aside and make a decision to learn to like it. This can be achieved with a strategic plan or by outsourcing it to a professional.

Without clarity around where your audience spend time online, you may as well be blindfolded. And if you can't find your potential customer, you're not going to get any business.

4. How?

How are you going to communicate with your ideal clients? Your brand's core values will help determine your voice (and by 'voice', we mean the tone you'll take when you communicate). Perhaps your brand dictates a friendly tone, an advisory tone, a big sister tone, or a controversial tone. Whether you do your social media yourself, have a team member or various team members executing it, or you outsource to a specialist, **Get Clear** on what your voice is, so that there's consistency in your brand.

You might have between three and five value statements that you've taken the time to **Get Right**. But do your staff know what they are? Does your marketing person know what they are? A style guide can be useful for your business. As well as your brand's voice, also specify how your logo should be

used, what corporate colours should be chosen, and what fonts should be used in graphics.

Some of these guidelines won't be relevant to certain platforms. For instance, platforms such as LinkedIn don't allow for variations in font type, size or colour, but this doesn't stop you from incorporating a brand style in the graphics, documents and other media you're uploading to your profile or page.

5. What?

What do you want to achieve from your social media? *What* outcomes are you looking for? Many people will say it's sales, but in reality, some time is likely to elapse between someone connecting with you, realising they've got a problem you can fix, and then being ready to purchase from you. In fact, they need to have between seven and nine touch points with you and your business until they're ready to buy from you specifically. Investing in relationship-building and creating valuable content will result in you being top of mind.

What metrics are you going to use to gauge your success? Is your success about brand awareness? Is it about building an audience? Is it about engagement? Or is about leads and conversions? You can measure likes, comments, messages, phone calls, meetings, or actual sales. **Get Clear** on what to measure and ensure it connects to your outcomes.

6. When?

When will you activate each part of your strategy? You might decide to focus on only one social media platform, or you might decide you're going to create a strategy across three platforms. But are you going to action them all at once?

If you're already using a Facebook page, a LinkedIn profile, or YouTube, start by establishing your audience are actually there. When you're sure that you're in the right space, review your platform set-up. Part of your strategy should be to ensure each one is well branded and using the right keywords to match your audience. Only then can you establish a timeframe around optimising each account and a guide on when to use them.

If, on the other hand, you're only getting started with your social media, or you're refocusing and parking some of your platforms, create a timeline to manage when and how you activate them.

Also, when are you going to create and publish the content for each platform? There are two types of created content: content that's created from scratch, and content that's repurposed from existing published content. Create a plan to create or repurpose your content, publish it, and then promote it.

A big part of content marketing is timing. Often missed by businesses is the need to market the content at times that will ensure maximum exposure and engagement. Some people may see your content when it's published on an ad-hoc basis, but not everyone is sitting at their computer at the time you happen to press 'publish'. Schedule it for a time your audience is online. Also try publishing on LinkedIn and promoting via Twitter to engage two different audiences.

Another 'when' to consider is when will you manage your engagement? When your audience engage with you over your content, you need to engage back. Think of when you have a real conversation with someone at a networking event and you say something to start a discussion; it's polite to respond to that person when they reply to you. The same conversational skills apply online. If you share an article and someone takes the time to add a comment to your article, it's

good manners and good social practice to thank them for their comment. Maybe ask another question to further engage with them; a conversation goes a long way in building a relationship.

The final ‘when’ that you might want to think about is: when do you decide to proactively engage with your ideal customer on their own social media platform? To build a relationship with a potential ideal client, first create a plan to monitor them. Once you’ve gathered an idea about how they operate online, engage with them by commenting on their page or profile. I'm not talking about adding a comment to say, “Read my article” or “Buy my stuff” with a link to your product or page. I'm talking about adding value to their conversation or thanking them or asking a question.

7. **Was it worth it?**

This question is the one that's often missed: were your efforts worth it? Work out which platforms are working for you, what type of content is engaging your audience, and what on earth you’re going to measure. If your focus is brand awareness, you might measure the number of your page likes, followers, connections or subscribers, because these are your audience-building metrics. If you're at the stage where you're looking to engage with your audience, you might instead measure comments, likes and shares, because that's where there’s social engagement.

Some of the measurements are within the social media platform itself. Facebook pages, for example, have analytics, which show you who your audience is, what type of content they engage with, and what time of day they're online. LinkedIn has similar tools, particularly for company pages. On your LinkedIn profile, some of the statistics you might look for are profile views, connection requests, or the number of people engaging with your content.

Other measurements can come from offline methods, and these can be more challenging to capture. When people call you, for example, make sure you ask them how they heard about you or where they've seen you. It might have been that they first noticed you on LinkedIn or Facebook, but they've gone to your website before they've called you. Work out what's working for you and measure it.

Take the time to get it right

Building a social media strategy can take time. If you're worried that you don't yet have all this information – about your customers, their habits, who they are, and what their problems are – please don't stress. Better now than never.

Start with research. Put together a survey, or work with a specialist, so you can get into the heads of your ideal client and work out what problems they have. Find out what's stopping them from engaging with your services right now. Also, gather some intelligence around the problem, so you can create content to connect and build trust.

We're living in an era of social media and digital connection; this is where the opportunities are and it's important for your business to there. Most of your clients are on some form of social media and the numbers are growing each year. When you're in the city, take a look around. The people who are walking with their heads down on mobile devices are most likely on social media. They're on social media on the train. They're on social media watching TV. They're even on social media in bed. Wherever they are, they're using social media tools and consuming content in some form or another.

You need to be where your customers are, so take the time to build your plan, implement and manage it. And if you can't

build a strategy by yourself, then outsource it. Find somebody who has the time, skills and expertise to work out the right platforms and activities for your business.

How do I know it's going to work for me?

Well, there are no guarantees. That's a fact. But although we can't guarantee that social media will achieve all your business goals in the desired timeframe, we can certainly make an informed guess. By looking at your statistics and analytics, and seeing what's working for you, right now, we can predict your success or failure.

You need to know what you're measuring, where to look, which tools to use, and what metrics matter the most. Vanity metrics are 'likes', 'followers' and 'subscribers', and by themselves, aren't altogether useful. From these statistics, you don't actually know if these people care enough about your business to engage. Focus on strategies to entice them to engage with your content by commenting, clicking through to your website or downloading a free resource; then, measure these metrics of engagement. These statistics will tell you a lot more about your customer and what they connect with online.

Social media is always changing, so review your metrics often and then adapt your strategy accordingly. One small change on LinkedIn, for example, can greatly impact the way your audience interact with you. Also, your audience will change as they move along the customer journey. They will start as complete strangers (albeit friendly strangers), but as they get to know you and your brand, they either become more aligned with your content or more distant. Looking at what type of content is working gives you the feedback you need to adapt. It also enables you to establish real relationships and build a community of people who love what you do.

GET CLEAR

Map out a plan to get crystal clear on what you want to achieve and how you propose to get there.

Share your plan with us via email at GetGoodOrGetOff@gmail.com

Chapter 9

Get On With It

Ailsa Page

"Every great journey starts with a single step."
Lao Tzu

Well done! You've made it to the final chapter. And you know what? This chapter is all about making the big decision. Here, we will clarify your future actions around social media, and identify the steps to either **Get Good** or **Get Off**. Whether you work to improve your outcomes, or decide to save yourself some time and money, things will change from here on in. How exciting.

Of course, you don't actually have to do anything. You could just keep doing what you're doing and keep getting the same old outcomes.

"If nothing changes, nothing changes. If you keep doing what you're doing, you're going to keep getting what you're getting. You want change, make some."
Courtney C Stevens

Your body has three natural responses when under stress; you're probably familiar with at least two. There's the 'flight' response, which is when a person runs away from a stressful situation, and there's the 'fight' response, which is when we stay to fight the danger. The third and lesser known response is the 'freeze' response. The freeze response usually occurs under trauma or extreme stress and is when your body does nothing — that's right, absolutely nothing.

Social media has caused a lot of stress to business owners, individuals, corporations, and not-for-profits, and many of

us do absolutely nothing to change the situation. Now, unless doing nothing is an *active* decision, the stress remains.

Don't freeze

We're a little worried that some of you might choose to freeze. Although natural, it's happening way too much in businesses at the moment and becoming detrimental to social media. Perhaps the freeze response is happening as part of an overall overwhelm that people are experiencing at present. Maybe it's stressful times, maybe it's information overload, or maybe there are just too many marketing options to contemplate.

Often, when there are too many options to get our head around, we tend to bury our heads in the sand. The key problem with this is that no decisions are being made. Time ticks on by, and businesses are stuck in the same pattern, getting the same results.

What this book is here to do is encourage you to take some action. Remember, as Courtney Stevens says, "*If nothing changes, nothing changes*". If you put your decision-making around social media aside, time goes on. In fact, a year or two might go past, and still there's no decision. If, in the meantime, you continue to do bad social media, it's going to damage your brand. A non-decision is a non-commitment and sends a weak signal to your audience. You cannot afford a weak online presence when so many people are checking you out online.

You must have a strong presence. You must commit to marketing that's going to work. If your main form of marketing is through social media, then it's important to make it work. Yes, you can opt to freeze, but what will you achieve? Just remember that every great journey starts with

a single step, so it's important to take action – even if it's just to decide to postpone your decision for a short while.

So, let's look at the other two choices, so you can make the right choice for you and your business. If you want a different outcome to the one you've got, then it's time to make a decision.

Take flight

Choosing the flight response means to **Get Off** your social media, and that's absolutely okay for you to choose. The whole premise of this book is that if you're not doing well on social media, save your time, money and effort, and just **Get Off**. Just leave it be. Don't do bad social media. Just give it a rest.

After reading this book, you might now have peace of mind that your feelings of stress and being over it are not the way it's meant to be. If you haven't been getting the results on social media that you desire, and you can't see the value in fixing it, then it's definitely time to **Get Off**.

Take the newfound time to get your sanity back, gain some perspective, and rejuvenate. Who knows? You may decide to **Get Back On** at a later time or... you may not. Either way, your decision has been made, and in making the decision, your stress will automatically reduce. It's also important to **Get Off** social media if you're not doing it very well. The damage to brand is a real risk.

And remember, there are many different ways to **Get Off** social media. The first option is to downsize your commitment by reducing the amount of social media platforms you are on. Simply **Get Off** the ones that aren't working for you, **Get Off** the ones you don't like, and **Get Off** the ones that aren't attracting your target market. You

might decide to focus on just one platform and do it well. Very few businesses do more than one or two social platforms well, so why even bother to try more.

Don't forget, you can also park everything. Rather than go in and delete all your profiles, deactivate them instead, so they're not visible to the public. This gives you the flexibility of not having to start from scratch if you decide to come back at a future stage and reignite them.

And if you choose to downsize or park your accounts, just think what else you can do to achieve results. Of course, you still want to get all the things you were hoping to get from social media —sales goals, brand awareness, and leads — but now, focus on other forms of marketing to achieve these objectives. There are so many other opportunities and methods for you to market your business these days. I always say to people that if they don't like online networking, then try offline networking instead. You can get just as good results offline, particularly if you learn to do it well.

If you decide not to do social media anymore, it's not the end of the world. You may need to work a bit harder in some of your other marketing areas, but so what? You can do that. Particularly, if other marketing areas excites you.

"Without promotion, something terrible happens — NOTHING!"
P.T. Barnum

Stay and fight

How about now you've read the book and seen all the options, you decide you're going to fight to **Get Good** on social media. Well, good for you! It's worth it. And with that attitude, you'll get great results. If you're going to commit to social media, then Getting Good is the only option. Do it well for everyone's sake. Get the results you desire.

In this book, we've given you lots of ways to **Get Good**, so now it's over to you. A new understanding of your situation and why you're doing it will engender commitment in your decision. For you to do business well, it's so important to understand *why* you're doing it.

Remember, the first step is to develop your strategy. This is really, really important. It's the No. 1 task. We've given you the tools; now, go and find a strategy that works for you. You can do it by yourself or you can get an expert in to help you, but it's always *you* who's best placed to drive your own social media strategy.

The next step is to learn how to execute your strategy. So, learns the skills you need and step up, or if you decide that this task would be better suited to someone else, again, get someone else to do it. If it's a lack of time that's holding you back, remember you don't have to learn or do everything. Just get the why and what, and then get someone else to do the rest.

"You never change your life until you step out of your comfort zone; change begins at the end of your comfort zone."
Roy T. Bennett

GET CLEAR

Alright, you can do it! You *can* make the decision to **Get Good** or **Get Off**, and you'll feel so much better when you do. Turn the page to commit to your decision, and it's done – no more procrastination, no more worry, just strategic action.

Decision Time

What are you going to do? Tick the boxes in the table below:

	GET GOOD		GET OFF
☐	Develop your strategy	☐	Park everything
☐	Learn how to execute	☐	Downsize – focus on one or two platforms only
☐	Outsource	☐	Do something else – focus on other marketing

Get Good or Get Off Agreement

Starting today, I _________________ (insert name),

agree to GET GOOD or GET OFF social media (circle what is appropriate for you) and use my time, money and energy more effectively.

The first step I need to take is __________________

____

____

____

____

____

____

I need support with ____________________

____

____

Sign: ____________________________________

Date: ____________________________________

Now share this with us to stay accountable.

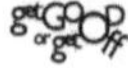

CONCLUSION

Well done for reaching the final page! We hope you've reached a decision. Whether it's to **Get Good** at your social media, or **Get Off** and free yourself from the shame and stress of bad social media, you'll finally be able to invest your energy wisely.

Social media is an incredible phenomenon in the world of business, but we understand it can be stressful. This book is designed to help simplify this highly complex area of marketing. We've covered the successful components of a good social media strategy, what can work, and what to avoid.

Now you're at the end of the book, we would love to hear what your decision is. Share what you discovered, what you have agreed to and what you plan to do now.

If you've chosen to **Get Good**, and develop your strategy and execute it, we're here to help. We can also provide recommendations to those wanting to outsource the work.

Alternatively, if you want help **Getting Off**, Jo can help with the technical side of things and Ailsa can help with your alternate marketing strategy.

Whatever you choose, we're here to support you.

Make sure you tell us your success stories. We'd love to hear your feedback on the book and your ah-ha moments.

Email us at: GetGoodOrGetOff@gmail.com

GET SOCIAL

#GetGoodOrGetOff

We would love you to share a selfie with your book to your favourite social media platform, tagging us and using #GetGoodOrGetOff

Follow Jo Saunders

Facebook	/WildfireSocialMarketing
LinkedIn	/in/josaunders
Twitter	@joatwildfire
Instagram	@wildfiresm

Follow Ailsa Page

Facebook	/AP.Marketing.Works
LinkedIn	/in/ailsapage
Twitter	@AilsaPage
Instagram	@ailsajpage

GET MORE VALUE

If you've found the information in this book useful and would now like guidance and support on your marketing journey, we would love to chat with you about how we can help.

We have the following book offers:

1. **Develop a Digital Strategy eBook**
   by Ailsa Page
   » http://bit.ly/2qDQW5a

2. **DIY LinkedIn Profile Audit Program**
   by Jo Saunders
   » http://bit.ly/GGOGOLI

3. **Join our online program**
   Gain access to templates, resources, and any updates to this book in PDF format
   » http://bit.ly/GetGoodVault

You can also book us to speak at your next event on the topic of the book, or our individual topics (refer to our websites), or hire us to develop your social media strategy. Ailsa will work on your brand marketing strategy, while Jo will work on your platform strategy. With the dynamic duo at your disposal, just imagine how much can be achieved!

Contact us at: GetGoodOrGetOff@gmail.com

GET TO KNOW THE AUTHORS

Ailsa Page

Known as the marketing dynamo, Ailsa Page knows business and knows what it takes to be successful. With over twenty years' experience in marketing, running her own businesses and helping other businesses improve their bottom line, Ailsa is regularly called upon by government and businesses for her expertise.

An award-winning business owner, Certified Speaking Professional, and former judge on the Telstra Business Awards and Women's Awards, Ailsa is a regular contributor to MYOB 'The Pulse' and Inside Small Business. A fellow of the Australian Marketing Institute and a Certified Practising Marketer, Ailsa runs her own marketing agency, AP Marketing Works, providing marketing strategy, advice, coaching, education, and implementation services to small and medium business.

She has authored the Shoe String Marketing Kit for Small Business and The Year I Owned a Wine Shop, and is a featured presenter in Victoria's Small Business Festival. Ailsa is known for her infectious enthusiasm and for being the 'city chick' who understands marketing in regional and rural Australia.

Phone: +61 (0)419 546 159
Email: ailsa@apmarketingworks.com.au
Web: www. apmarketingworks.com.au

GET TO KNOW THE AUTHORS

Jo Saunders

Jo Saunders is an international LinkedIn expert, digital marketing strategist, and social media educator who's been helping individuals connect and communicate since the early nineties through pen and paper, events, and now, social media

Known for demystifying the complexities of LinkedIn and other social media tools, Jo provides training, mentoring, and consulting to individuals, business owners, marketing managers and teams. She helps her clients communicate their brand message, market their services, showcase their talent, and build relationships in the era of social business.

Jo has trained thousands of people around the world to use LinkedIn more effectively and was named one of the top two hundred LinkedIn practitioners in the world. She was an Australian Web Awards judge for three years, wrote two chapters for the book, Getting Your Business LinkedIn, and was ranked No. 5 on Klout's list of LinkedIn experts.

Check out her LinkedIn profile to discover more »
https://au.linkedin.com/in/josaunders

Phone: +61 (0)422 431 039
Email: jo@wildfiresm.com
Web: www.wildfiresocialmarketing.com

HAVE YOU ENJOYED THIS BOOK?

We would love you to write a review or record a quick video with your book to say hi and tell us what you enjoyed about our book. Here are a few additional reviews from our readers;

"*What Jo and Ailsa have produced with Get Good or Get Off is a practical guide covering the type of questions that anybody in business should be asking themselves today. This is no rosy picture written for other social media marketers, but instead it's a book written with business leaders in mind. A highly recommended read.*"

Marcus Boswell »Social Selling Consultant » UK

"*Let's face it, we live in a fast-paced world where being good at what you do separates you from the pack. Filled with practical tips and a great perspective, Get Good or Get Off takes the reader on a journey of discovery on how to Get Good at social media. Whether we like or not, social media is now an integral part of marketing, and getting good at it allows you to stand out from your competitors; so Get Good or Get Off.*"

Christina Cabrera » Money Mentor to Woman & Financial Wellness Specialist » Australia

"Get Good or Get Off; that is exactly what I like about Jo Saunders — she tells it like it is. In this book, co-authored by Ailsa Page, you'll get drawn right in. I finished the book in one go, only putting it down for a quick run to the loo and to grab another cup of tea.

Saunders and Page help you identify if social media is even what you need. If you decide it is for you, then the clear outlined do's and don'ts guide you into your own effective and, above all, authentic social media presence.

Why should you read this book? One: it is a book. As much as my business is online, I am a sucker for print on paper. Two: it has the right balance between actionable steps and entrepreneurial stories. Heck, Kate Lister is featured. Need I say more? Three: this book offers one of the easiest yet most engaging ways I've come across to set up your social media strategy."

Petra Fisher » LinkedIn Storyteller » The Netherlands

"I was expecting to spend hours reading a technical book. To my surprise, it was an easy read. I particularly liked how Jo and Alisa focused on the why. I now know that I want to focus on connecting and building relationships with people. I want to join in their conversations and share freely without any expectations. It's not about selling.

The big takeaway for me is the importance of being consistent and keeping the focus on giving and sharing information that my clients or potential clients need. Being on social media is not about being all things to all people."

Violet Dhu » Corporate Communication Experts » Australia

"Jo and Ailsa offer excellent tips and ideas on how to stand out in the online arena. They raise interesting and thought-provoking issues around brand and perception, and provide great information on how to engage your target audience."

Dale Rees-Bevan » Speakersbank » Australia

GET THANKFUL

The idea for this book was hatched at the 2014 Professional Speakers Australia Convention, where we met for the first time. Professional Speakers Australia consistently encourage us — both as speakers and as trainers —to better develop our business skills related to professional speaking.

Thank you to the many individuals and businesses we have worked with across Australia who have provided so much insight and inspiration. To our network of professionals, who motivate and support us, and to the many business owners we work with, know that you have contributed to the ideas in this book in some way.

Given that we live on opposite sides of the country, it was important to hang out in the same place from time to time to bring the book to life. Thanks to our partners and family for the support and patience, and the town of Marysville for providing us with a beautiful haven to create this book.

Thanks to those who read the draft and provided feedback, to Tim Hughes for writing our Foreword, and to our early readers who wrote testimonials. Thanks also to our network who have shared their publishing experiences.

To our publishing team; a special thanks to Eleanor Mulder from Elephant Edits for making sure our message makes sense; Ming Chong for your creative ideas; Jeremy Phillips for coming up with the perfect by-line; and to Silvia Tjong for bringing Jo's sketches to life.

This book is already a workshop and keynote, and we thank Professional Speakers Australia for having faith to host our first joint workshop at the National Conference in 2017.

www.ingramcontent.com/pod-product-compliance
Lightning Source LLC
Chambersburg PA
CBHW020837210326
41598CB00019B/1931

* 9 7 8 0 9 8 0 5 4 1 1 2 0 *